# THE DRUMMER

## 100 YEARS OF RHYTHMIC POWER AND INVENTION

Edited by **Adam Budofsky**
Designed by **Michele Heusel**

Assistant Editors:
**Michael Dawson**
**Michael Parillo**

D1159436

**Published by Modern Drummer Publications**

Hadas

ISBN: 978-1-4234-7660-3

Copyright © 2006
Modern Drummer Publications

Published by
Modern Drummer Publications
12 Old Bridge Road
Cedar Grove, NJ 07009

Library Of Congress
Cataloging-in-Publication
has been applied for.

Printed at Walsworth Publishing Company,
U.S.A.

Fifth Edition June 2016.

Visit Modern Drummer Online at
www.moderndrummer.com.

1 0 9 8 7 6 5

EXCLUSIVELY DISTRIBUTED BY
HAL•LEONARD®
CORPORATION
7777 W. BLUEMOUND RD. P.O. BOX 13819 MILWAUKEE, WI 53213

# Foreword

## by Chad Smith

**W**e've all heard more than a few drummer jokes, usually involving some kind of drooling caveman who can't count, can't keep a job, and can't find the keys when he locks himself into the van. Drummer jokes have never bothered me. I love a good laugh, and if joking about us makes our fellow musicians feel more important, I say let the baby have his bottle—we can take it.

When it comes right down to it, we always get the last laugh anyway. Why? Because we are truly indispensable musicians: We provide the bedrock, the very foundation that so many forms of music are built upon. Our rhythms give life to the melody, the lyric, the song. They give the music emotion, excitement, tension, and at the very least, they give everyone something to tap their toes to. Drummers supply the heartbeat, the pulse to the rest of the band. It's been said that a good drummer can make a mediocre band sound great. It's true. Let's face it: Those other guys are nothing without us!

But that's not why most of us become drummers. For me, it began when I was seven years old, banging away on overturned ice cream tubs with Lincoln Logs. Before long I was rocking out on a real drumset, doing my best to imitate my heroes, the players who helped make me the drummer I am today. I still listen to those same players for inspiration.

My own drumming has taken me on a lifelong journey that has surpassed even my wildest dreams. I've been fortunate enough to have met (and even played with) many of my childhood heroes—the ones who influenced me to play drums in the first place. I've gotten to see firsthand how positive and powerful a force music, and especially rhythm, can be. There's nothing like the exhilaration of having an audience—I don't care what size it is—clapping their hands or stomping their feet to the groove you are playing. When The Chili Peppers played

Joan & Curt Smith

in London's Hyde Park in 2004, I came back onstage before the encore and played a few bars of beats from some of my favorite songs. Each beat brought a wave of recognition and applause from the crowd; we were all speaking in the language of rhythm, and it was one of the biggest rushes I've ever experienced.

I've come to believe that the best drummers are the ones who imprint the music with their own personal mark while still supplying the vital elements of time, feel, and emotion. This is the common thread that all of the drummers in this book share. We live to serve the music and to feed the fire of creativity for ourselves, for other musicians, and hopefully for the listener. When that happens, it's the greatest thrill of all. And *that* is no joke.

Since 1989, Chad Smith and his band, The Red Hot Chili Peppers, have earned worldwide success, garnering respect from the critics and the devotion of a rabid fan base that continues to grow with every record. They have sold millions of records and won Grammy Awards in 1992 and 1999. Chad has won numerous awards, including Rock Drummer Of The Year in *Modern Drummer*'s 2005 Readers Poll. As a session drummer, he has played with John Fogerty, The Wu-Tang Clan, Johnny Cash, and The Dixie Chicks. His popular in-store clinics and instructional DVDs support the claim that Chad is one of the best drum ambassadors of our time.

The drummer is the center of gravity for any group, no matter what kind of music they play. In the studio or on stage, the drums are the first instrument the engineer focuses on because everything else is built around them.

—Tommy James

Let me paraphrase Lenny Bruce: If the drums are swingin', the band's swingin'—even if it's not. If the drums ain't swingin', the band ain't swingin'—even if it is. —Paul Shaffer (music director, *The Late Show With David Letterman*)

## MY WIFE HAS A TROUBLING FONDNESS FOR DRUMMERS.
### —ROB THOMAS

A drummer certainly needs to be something of a shaman. He also needs the power of a ringmaster, as well as total self-confidence unspoiled by something like reading books. (Thinking may make him insecure.) Only exceptional master drummers like Jaki Liebezeit can afford such an exquisite occupation as studying Sanskrit without getting confused.

—Irmin Schmidt (Can)

**"We're ALL drummers. When I'm working the strings with my right hand, I'm playing a drum part. Rhythm is involved with everything. It's just different perspectives on the same thing. We're trying to make these machines laugh and cry."**

**—Mike Watt**

THE DRUMMER IS THE MOST IMPORTANT MUSICIAN IN ANY BAND. HE MAKES IT HAPPEN BY THE FEEL HE BRINGS TO THE ENSEMBLE. A GREAT DRUMMER DRIVES THE BUS, MAKES THE STOPS, PICKS UP THE SOLOS, AND ORCHESTRATES THE VOCALS. HE OR SHE CAN MAKE OR BREAK A GREAT BAND.
—PETER FRAMPTON

I like to experiment with drum sounds. On *Raindogs* in NYC, I wanted a big backbeat for the song "Singapore," which I couldn't get with the drumkit. Lucky for me, it was trash day and I remembered this chest of drawers on the sidewalk outside of the studio. So we dragged it in, and Michael Blair hit it with a 2x4 that I just happened to have with me at the time. He kept hitting away in this live chamber, and it was like *heaven*. But then he suggested, "Let's sample the sound and save the furniture." I considered that an attempt to shirk his duty, a reluctance to knuckle down and keep it raw. And I told him so. He hit it as hard as he could on each backbeat of this four-minute song. Well, as you can hear, he had no trouble beating that chest for the entire song. He chopped it down to kindling without ever missing the beat.
Now *that's* what I call timing.

—Tom Waits

The drums set the pace for what everyone else is doing, and that's the whole feel of the song. It might be the song that's written, but how it's going to come across as a finished product has *so* much to do with the drums. A lot of people don't realize this.
—Slash (Guns N' Roses/Velvet Revolver)

HAVING A DRUMMER LIKE BILL BRUFORD, WITH HIS TECHNICAL PRECISION, HELPED TO GOVERN US ALL. WE COULD HAVE HAD A MORE ORDINARY DRUMMER, BUT IT COULDN'T HAVE WORKED AS WELL. HE WAS HOLDING THE BAND TOGETHER. HE WAS LIKE A BRITISH FRANK ZAPPA. HE ALWAYS HAD STUFF TO SAY, AND HE WAS ALWAYS ON THE EDGE, AND HE WAS NOT PREDICTABLE. AND IT WASN'T JUST HIS MUSIC. IT WAS HIS THINKING. THERE WAS A FLOWERING.
—STEVE HOWE (YES)

# THE DRUMS ARE THE HEART, GUTS, AND SOUL, THE DRIVING FORCE BEHIND THE MUSIC.
## —BILLY IDOL

**NOTHING GIVES ME AN ADRENALINE RUSH LIKE TWO HOURS ON MY DRUMS. IS IT WEIRD I THINK MY FLOOR TOM HAS SEXIER LEGS THAN ANY WOMAN I'VE EVER MET?**
—DAMIEN FAHEY (MTV VJ)

Once upon a time, rock 'n' roll was dance music. And in the Underground Garage it still is! So that makes the drummer extremely important, second only to the songwriters. We must always keep in mind that the best drummers in the world (and guitar players and everybody else) are only as good as their ability to serve the song. So what do Ringo, Charlie Watts, Al Jackson, Roger Hawkins, Earl Palmer, and Hal Blaine have in common? The perfect fill at the perfect time—and knowing when no fill at all serves a song best.

—Little Steven (Bruce Springsteen)

It's all drums. A piano is eighty-eight drums. Actually, the possibilities of drums in a piano are limitless. A guitar, a hundred and something. Violins are drums with strings attached that you play with a bow. But it's all attack and tone and overtone. Resonance.

—T-Bone Burnett (artist, producer)

**THE PERFECT DRUMMER PLAYS WITH A RICH TONE. HE HAS EXCELLENT TECHNIQUE, A KEEN UNDERSTANDING OF FORM, A GREAT SENSE OF VARIETY, AND A GREATER ABILITY TO MAKE ACCURATE, INFORMED DECISIONS IN REAL TIME. MOST IMPORTANTLY, THE PERFECT DRUMMER PLAYS AT THE PROPER VOLUME FOR EACH MUSICAL SITUATION. MOST TIMES THE PERFECT DRUMMER IS SUPPORTIVE, OTHER TIMES DEMANDING, AND ON OCCASION OVERBEARING. THE PERFECT DRUMMER UNDERSTANDS HOW TO SUPPORT THE ENSEMBLE AND THE SOLOIST WITH LOVE, CARE, AND SINCERITY. ELVIN JONES WAS THE PERFECT DRUMMER.**
—DELFEAYO MARSALIS (PRODUCER, TROMBONIST, BANDLEADER)

**REAL DRUMS, PLAYED BY REAL DRUMMERS: AN ART OF SOUND THAT I'VE BEEN ATTEMPTING TO CAPTURE FOR THIRTY-FIVE YEARS. EVEN GETTING *CLOSE* TO THE REALITY AND HUMANITY ARE BEYOND MEASURE.**
—JACK DOUGLAS (PRODUCER)

Some Neanderthal was probably nervously tapping on a sheep skull and thought, "This kind of sounds good. I wonder what happens if I make the eye holes a bit bigger…." And at that point, somebody started forever tuning their *%#@ing drums. "Bom bom bom, bom bom bom, bom bom bom—Hold on, I'll be with you in few minutes!—bom bom bom, bom bom bom…." Yeah, Neanderthal drummers. But I say that with fondness: Gene Krupa, John Bonham, and everybody else—there's something pretty animal about drummers everywhere.

—Ian Anderson (Jethro Tull)

It's tough being "the drummer." It's up to you to lay down the groove, then hold everybody else together. And as if that's not enough, all the other guys in the band think you're difficult or crazy! And then, they start with the jokes: "What has three legs and a prick? A drum stool." It ain't easy being the drummer.

—Mark Hudson (producer)

**TWO GIRLS ARE WALKING ALONG WHEN THEY HEAR, "PSST…DOWN HERE!" THEY BOTH LOOK DOWN AND SEE A FROG SITTING BESIDE THE ROAD. SUDDENLY THE FROG SAYS, "IF YOU KISS ME, I'LL TURN INTO A WORLD-FAMOUS DRUMMER AND MAKE YOU BOTH RICH AND FAMOUS!" THE TWO GIRLS LOOK AT EACH OTHER, AND ONE OF THEM REACHES DOWN, GRABS THE FROG, AND STUFFS IT INTO HER POCKET. THE OTHER GIRL SAYS, "WHAT DID YOU DO THAT FOR?" THE FIRST REPLIES, "I'M NOT STUPID, I KNOW A TALKING FROG IS WORTH HEAPS MORE THAN A FAMOUS DRUMMER ANY DAY!"**
—BRYAN ADAMS

F**king drummers…we need the poor bastards if only to have them be the butt of all of those jokes! Seriously, I can't imagine a world without drummers. They are the glue and inspiration that holds it all together.
—Eddie Kramer (producer)

G race, authority, and character. If you're going to be judged on how well you hit something, *those* are the measures. Not how hard you hit. Not how fast. But how artfully, how deliberately, and with how much personality.

The drummers you'll be reading about in this book elevated the music they played—and the consciousness of those who heard it—because they had something to say and the confidence to say it. They didn't follow, nor did they force. They exuded strength, mesmerized, and told a tale. They convinced us to dance. They reminded us of our connection to the earth. They expanded our perception of the complexities of life. They made us feel good.

Once upon a time—and sometimes still—you'd get laughed at for describing drummers in such hoity-toity terms. The butt of a thousand (generally bad) jokes, drummers for ages had to suffer the indignity of being considered third-class musicians.

It's hard to say exactly why this is. Maybe we're just easy targets. We sit when we play, so we're already on the losing side of a power play. We're usually toward the back of the stage, in the shadows, without a microphone to say clever things through, or a sexy low-slung guitar to swing around. Then there's that "hitting" thing. Somehow, when your job involves striking an object to get a sound out of it, people assume you're a simplistic communicator.

"Whatever," the drumming community collectively sighs. "We know the real deal."

And to be sure, there *is* a drumming community (and it does collectively sigh on occasion, like when drum machines first arrived on the scene). The brotherhood of drummers is not just some marketing idea the publishers of this book concocted thirty years ago, when *Modern Drummer* magazine was founded. It's simply a reality we tapped into, and one that we promoted with gusto.

While guitarists often guard their playing secrets like Gollum and his ring, drummers readily share what they know. This is not just a romantic notion, either. The couple thousand drummers who trek to *Modern Drummer*'s Festival Weekend every year, to meet and ask questions of their heroes and share their experiences with fellow drummers—these people are an undeniably unique subset of the music community. If I had a dime for each time I overheard someone at MD Fest say to a buddy, "You know, guitarists would never do this sort of thing...."

It's in that spirit of sharing the wisdom of our drumming gods—and of giving well-deserved credit to the most misunderstood person on every dinky stage in every dinky bar—that we present to you *The Drummer: 100 Years Of Rhythmic Power And Invention*. Fueled by an insatiable urge to hit things in time, and feel them hit us back...addicted to the sound of resonating objects crashing into each other...spurred on by the sweat and inspiration a good rip around the kit provides.... The drummer with the extra pair of sticks forever in his trunk and a bad habit of tapping out paradiddles at the dinner table—this is a special person indeed, and a member of a special club.

Drummer, we salute you. This book is for you.

Adam Budofsky
Editor

# The View From Here

Playing drums opened up the world for me, when I was ten years old. Wanting to be in a band felt exciting, like I would begin a long adventure. And even though guitarists and singers got the most attention, the drum chair, being in "the driver's seat," looked like the place to be. The best view in the house.

The feel of real acoustic drums was incredibly attractive. Physical. Powerful. It still feels that way. Even today, if I strike my wonderful 1965 Ludwig SuperClassic 9x13 rack tom in the right way, it sounds beautiful. Full of life and energy. It has the Black Diamond Pearl finish (as close to Ringo's kit as I could get from my local music store in Virginia), so it looks beautiful, too. Good vibrations in the literal sense. As a kid, if I hit it harder, it got louder. Such power I had then, in my own ten-year-old hands.

The fact that the first band I played in (during 7th grade) was with two very cute, smart, guitar-playing girls didn't hurt. They also sang like angels, so rehearsing with them in my parents' front room was not a chore, whatsoever.

I remember playing the lovely Kinks song "Tired Of Waiting" at a school party with Mary Anne and our other friend (whose name escapes me now). The entire class was swinging and swaying together. And it was a very useful "slow dance" song at the first signs of what I would soon call "puberty."

I was hooked.

I feel safe and protected when I play the drums. A story recently told to me by the very fabulous Jim Keltner supports that image. Actually, it's more a reflection on being a musician.

We were talking about growing up playing the drums. As in most every school, Jim's high school in Oklahoma had the usual separation of kids into different groups. The cool. The uncool. The jocks. The nerds. The bullies who beat up the nerds.

Jim told me he never got mobbed or picked on at school, because he played the drums. Being a musician was cool. He was respected, and the bullies left him alone.

This might sound like a small thing. But Jim said this meant a lot to him. To a kid growing up, getting positive feedback changes the way we look at ourselves, our self-confidence. We didn't have the neuropsychological research that is available now from major university studies that shows how the brain is wired to create and receive music. But we knew. We could feel it.

My version of "what playing the drums means to me" includes the fact that it was my ticket to fantastic travels, both near and far. My late father, Lee Blair, joined the Navy when he was in college, "to see the world" (as the recruiting poster said). I started playing drums and joining bands for the same reason.

Being able to meet so many different people in so many towns, cities, and countries has been amazing. That anyone enjoyed the music I would be playing was icing on an already tasty cake. The conversations, insights, and arguments have come in different languages, with people from different backgrounds and religions, all over the world.

A colleague of mine in Sweden has a son who is a young powerhouse of a drummer. It's inspiring to see *him* be so inspired. Maybe his drum journey will take him all over the planet too. I wish him well.

As The Grateful Dead said, "What a long, strange trip it's been." And worth every paradiddle I ever practiced.

On we go.

Michael Blair
Stockholm, Sweden

# All I Hear Is The Drummer

There are a lot of good bands with good drummers, but there are no great bands without a great drummer.

I don't remember who said that to me, but I never forgot it. I play just about every instrument better than I play the drums, yet when I go out to clubs to hear live music, my mind strips away each musician—one by one—until all I hear is the drummer. The singer may be the focus of a band, the guitar player the flash, the bassist the bottom, various instruments the flavor, but the drummer…the drummer is the one who can elevate the ensemble with energy, rhythm, tone. The right drummer can make a great band legendary. Do you remember what Nirvana sounded like before Dave Grohl joined? I do, and they weren't going to shake the world without him.

As a music writer, I listen to thousands of new CDs every year, and I can't tell you how many have been ruined for me by mediocre drumming. I'm biased against the overuse of 8th notes on the hi-hat, the aggressive pop of an overly torqued snare head, the thud of a poorly tuned floor tom. As a musician, I've felt the tidal pull of drummers who sped up mid-song, and I have tinnitus in the ear that had the misfortune of residing next to a brutally battered crash cymbal for lengthy periods of time. I've also had the good fortune of playing with drummers of impeccable taste whose main objective was to serve the song.

*Modern Drummer* magazine shines a spotlight on these underappreciated, oft joked about, and utterly essential musicians every month. The magazine has been bringing you tales from the kit for three decades, and now the *MD* editors are taking a new look at the music you love through the eyes and ears of those who propel it from the back of the stage.

*Modern Drummer* will always hold a special place in my heart. It was the first music publication that hired me—an opinionated kid with an insanely large record collection and an irrational love of drums—to scribe for them, and I'm honored to be here to advise you all to turn the page.

Meredith Ochs
Hoboken, NJ

# Gene Krupa

**Prime Gig**
Benny Goodman

**Classic Recording**
"Sing, Sing, Sing" (1937)

**Why We Worship**
the first drumming superstar •
bandleader who brought the drums
to the forefront • appeared in movies
(matinee-idol good looks) • driving
swing feel • exciting • impressive
tom-tom work • **Star**

# Buddy Rich

**Prime Gig**
Tommy Dorsey

**Classic Recording**
Mercy, Mercy (Buddy Rich Big Band, 1967)

**Why We Worship**
The most gifted drummer ever to pick up sticks
• tremendous technique (hands and feet) •
incredible combinations around kit • powerful
yet musical style • could play all styles of jazz,
but was the perfect big band drummer—and
knew it • **Attitude**

# Elvin Jones

**Prime Gig**
John Coltrane Quartet

**Classic Recording**
A Love Supreme (1964)

**Why We Worship**
totally original • passionate player • emotional approach
(beyond technique) • rhythmic elasticity • unique phrasing •
complex polyrhythms • over-the-barline • 18" bass drum •
small group master • **Touched by God**

# Tony Williams

**Prime Gig**
Miles Davis Quintet

**Classic Recording**
"Four" & More (1964)

**Why We Worship**
child prodigy (hired by Miles Davis at age
seventeen) • revolutionized jazz drumming
with advanced concepts (did the same for
fusion drumming) • blindingly fast ride cymbal
patterns • inventive solos • fast single bass
technique • yellow Gretsch kit • **Ego**

Colin Jones/Idols

# Keith Moon

**Prime Gig**
The Who

**Classic Recording**
Quadrophenia (1973)

**Why We Worship**
Played with wild abandon •
surprising, over-the-top fills •
created an energy and
excitement in music not
heard before—or since •
Premier drums • **Crazy**

# John Bonham

**Prime Gig**
Led Zeppelin

**Classic Recording**
Led Zeppelin IV (1971)

**Why We Worship**
power • the fattest groove ever •
huge, larger-than-life drum sound •
great soloist able to captivate large
rock crowds • impressive single bass
drum technique • Ludwig drums,
Paiste cymbals • **Swagger**

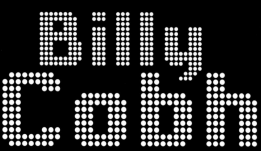

# Billy Cobham

**Prime Gig**
Mahavishnu Orchestra

**Classic Recording**
Spectrum (Billy Cobham, 1973)

**Why We Worship**
revolutionized drumming in 1970s
• legitimized matched grip • left-
hand lead, ambidextrous • huge
double (and sometimes *triple*) bass
kit • rudimental master • odd
meters • successful solo artist •
composer • **Creative**

# Steve

**Prime Gigs**
Paul Simon, Chick Corea

**Classic Recording**
"Aja" (Steely Dan, 1977)

**Why We Worship**
perfection in recording studio • fabulous
groove • inventive parts • popularized the
"controlled" '70s studio sound • great
technique—but keeps it hidden • black
Yamaha drums, Zildjian cymbals • suspended
floor toms • comfortable playing all styles,
yet still sounds unique • **Sensitive**

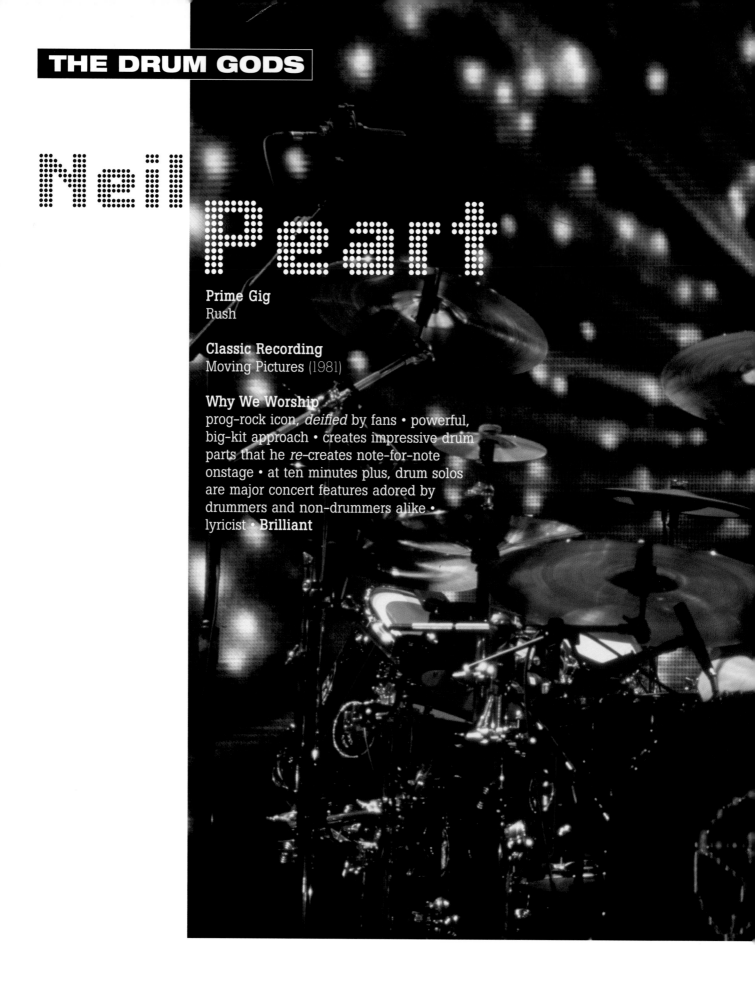

# Neil Peart

**Prime Gig**
Rush

**Classic Recording**
Moving Pictures (1981)

**Why We Worship**
prog-rock icon, *deified* by fans • powerful,
big-kit approach • creates impressive drum
parts that he *re*-creates note-for-note
onstage • at ten minutes plus, drum solos
are major concert features adored by
drummers and non-drummers alike •
lyricist • **Brilliant**

Ross Halfin/Idols

# Vinnie Colaiuta

**Prime Gig**
Frank Zappa

**Classic Recording**
Ten Summoner's Tales (Sting, 1993)

**Why We Worship**
the most technically advanced drummer
ever, with a deep understanding of
advanced rhythms and styles • handled
Zappa's crazed compositions, yet was
able to become a first-call LA studio
drummer • appreciates over-the-top
playing *and* simple grooving—and can do
both convincingly • **Explorer**

Deborah Stuer

# The Tools

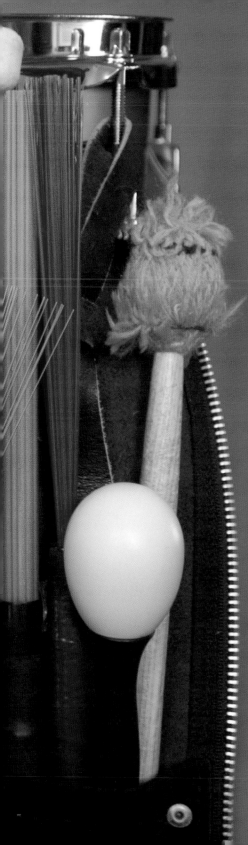

You hit a drum, it makes a sound. Simple.

Most drummers figure out pretty early in their development that there's more to the story. "Hmmm...that's interesting, when I hit it near the edge instead of in the middle, the sound changes. And if I hit the rim at the same time as the head—Whoa, that was cool!"

And so opens the first door of perception for the drummer. Getting a sound out of a drum *is* easy. Getting the sound you want, when you want it...well, that's quite another thing.

The drumstick is an extension of the hand. The hand is an extension of the mind. And a good drummer's mind never stops working. To sit behind a drumset is to be struck by the infinite possibilities of sound.

Over the years, drummers have employed every conceivable device to realize those possibilities. Brushes. Mallets. Knitting needles. Bundled dowels. Sticks made from hickory, maple, and carbon fiber. Fingertips. Each effect is different, and each results in a unique musical statement. The shocking crack of a snare rimshot. The mysterious wave of a mallet rolled on the edge of a cymbal.

From mind, to hand, to instrument. The drum is a universe of sound, waiting for a drummer to set it free.

**Chick Webb set the standard for how a drummer should drive a big band.**

# early jazz

## In the 20th Century,

by Will Romano

as jazz became more and more adventurous—mixing styles such as spirituals, blues, vaudeville, and folk—drummers realized they could, *and should*, play more than one pattern at once. The ancient African ritualistic concept of call & response, which was transferred to the continent of North America, had become imbedded in the rhythmic communication of the music.

Where it was once common practice to have more than one drummer for a piece of music—harking back to both the ancient African drum and European classical tradition—the single drummer emerged, with a new and vital role in the band. And enhanced by the advent of hardware technology, drummers more easily communicated with their bandmates.

By the 1930s, drumsets expanded in size and became ubiquitous, even if they were assembled piecemeal. Essentially, a drummer would have his 26" kick encased by a frame with wheels for easy load-in (or roll-in) and load-out. These frames, looking like something straight out of a Tim Burton film, had accessory arms that could be used by drummers in a surprisingly diverse number of ways, such as fastening temple blocks to posts jutting out from a metal "traps" tray resting just above the kick. Bent or gooseneck cymbal arms poked through any (and all) available spaces, as crescent moon–shaped cymbal stands circled overhead. This configuration proved to be an economical way for drummers to have a wide array of equipment at arm's length, and expand their rhythmic and sonic palette.

William Henry "Chick" Webb, the diminutive yet explosive drummer/bandleader who rose to prominence in the 1930s (and became an icon of the "swing" era), hammered out unique rhythmic phrases and voicings thanks to just such a contraption—the quirky forerunner to the modern-day rack system.

**SWING-ERA DRUMMERS HAD THE POWER TO PUSH OR CRUSH THE SOUND OF A BAND. ON THE BANDSTAND, THE DRUMMER HAD ULTIMATE CONTROL.**

# The Birth Of Swing

The most elemental, and perhaps necessary, instrument in early New Orleans street jazz was the drum. To be convinced, one need look no further than the second-line funeral parades brimming with marches, battle hymns, dirges, and Creole jazz. As Crescent City parades snaked through the streets, they coaxed bystanders to join the oddly joyous procession—whether the deceased was a close friend, respected musician, or complete stranger. It was the drummer, or drummers, who seduced passersby to let loose to the beat of their dance- and marching-band rhythms.

As a child, Louis Armstrong (a.k.a. Satchmo or Satchelmouth), one of the 20th century's most revered "pop" stars, was seduced by the exciting musical and rhythmic gumbo of New Orleans. The horn player's Hot Five band (including drummer Zutty Singleton, who wowed musicians and audiences alike with his mastery of the wire brushes) and Hot Seven band (which included Warren "Baby" Dodds) are generally seen as the peak of Armstrong's improvisational endeavors in the Roaring '20s. Due to leaps in recording technology, such as the switch from acoustical/horn-based recording to electrical recording with microphones, the drums on these mid-to-late-'20s sides are not relegated to the cellar.

It isn't much of a stretch to say that every modern jazz drummer owes a debt to Singleton—and perhaps even more so to Dodds. As part of Jelly Roll Morton's Red Hot Peppers and King Oliver's 1920s Creole Jazz Band, Dodds was among the first, if not *the* first, to employ a swing pattern beat on his "ride" cymbal. He would also use multiple sound sources to make his rhythmic points. His sense of timing, creative use of accents, and cymbal work are what mesmerized an up-and-coming drum wunderkind named Gene Krupa.

> **GENE KRUPA'S FLAMBOYANT, SYNCOPATED STYLE FORCED A GENERATION TO VIEW DRUMS NOT ONLY AS AN ESSENTIAL INSTRUMENT, BUT A LEAD ONE AS WELL.**

Others musicians were breaking boundaries, seemingly instinctually. After leaving King Oliver, Satchmo was tapped by Fletcher Henderson (who had a residency at New York's Roseland Ballroom). Henderson and Armstrong went on to create the joyous, boisterous sound of F. Scott Fitzgerald's "jazz age of the 1920s"—what our mind's ear conjures when recalling the sound of that time. With Louis Armstrong's slinky cornet phrasing, Coleman Hawkins' distinctive melodic tenor sax playing, drummer Joseph "Kaiser" Marshall's witty, well-placed cymbal accents (which spilled like bubbly foam from a champagne glass), and a healthy tendency to experiment with the elasticity of 4/4 time, Henderson's orchestra *killed* with swingin' numbers at the Roseland. Thus, the very term *swing* was born.

Meanwhile, up in Harlem, New York, swing was spotlighting musicians' expertise and their ability to get feets a-stomping on the dance floor. At the Savoy, innovative drummer and bandleader Chick Webb motivated and pushed his band from behind his enormous traps setup. Armstrong, Duke Ellington (who attracted curious white crowds to Harlem's Cotton Club with his "jungle music"), Webb, New Jersey-born Count Basie, and others further tinkered with the swing form and added to it—literally. Instead of five or seven pieces, bands now included an array of over a dozen musicians (more than one musician could be playing a particular instrument), creating a wall of intertwining, musical interplay.

Despite (or maybe because of) the stock market crash of 1929, music seemed to be as bright and loud as ever. With blaring ascending-descending horn and reed lines, swing became a musical force that helped many Americans through the tough economic years and, a few years later, the uncertainties of WWII. Swing, as the phrase goes, was king, at the record stores and in the dance halls.

## Jazz's Big Papa

If not for a drummer, jazz might look very different today.

New Orleans musician/drummer George Vetiala "Papa Jack" Laine, who some have dubbed the patriarch of jazz, was the most popular white musician in the Crescent City. He formed the first band to play ragtime music in 1888, and was a key figure in the development of the Dixieland jazz movement. Perhaps best remembered today as a bass drum player (though he did incorporate the snare into his bottom-end assault), Laine was a multi-instrumentalist of sorts, having played fife, whistle, string bass, and alto horn.

Laine employed such jazz pioneers as Joe "King" Oliver, Bunk Johnson, and Charles "Buddy" Bolden—in direct opposition to the segregation laws of the time. These musicians helped spread jazz to the far corners of the country. Members of Laine's Reliance Brass Band went on to form The Original Dixieland Jass Band—the first group, black or white, to record music of the jazz medium. How *much* of an impact Laine truly had on jazz's musical evolution and the styles of individual players might never be fully known. Still, it must be acknowledged that he was one of the most important behind-the-scenes jazz personalities in the late 19th and early 20th centuries.

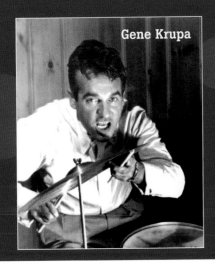
Gene Krupa

Cab Calloway's Cozy Cole was the first drummer noted for playing four different rhythmic figures simultaneously.

"Big" Sid Catlett had a major influence on the bop drummers of the 1940s.

# Drummer To The Forefront

The drummer's importance in swing music can't be overstated. Duke Ellington's "Black And Tan Fantasie" (with its yo-yo-ing sax lines, dreamy reed passages, and cry-baby, whinnying horns) is powered by Sonny Greer's incessant clanging. (The song is topped off by a Chopin-esque "Funeral March," making it a perfect mixture of the "low" and the "high" arts.)

Count Basie's "Jumpin' At the Woodside" (named after a Harlem hotel) is a rip-roaring, multi-voiced melodic romp that steadily builds to a spirited crescendo and features drummer Jo Jones' driving, sugary, subtle touch on hi-hats. By far one of the most beloved Basie songs, "Woodside" also showcases Jones as a quintessential swing man: He holds down the fort, which lets the other players go wherever they want to musically. (Though not as evident on this song, Jones became known for his accented cymbal patterns, which pushed and conversed with Basie's band.)

Swing-era drummers, whether smooth, rough, soft, or aggressive, had the power to push or crush the sound of a band. On the bandstand, the drummer had ultimate control. In fact, the man perched on his drum throne, arms flailing, was such an attraction, so integral to warming a dance hall (and getting people up and dancing), he became a kind of star—much to many a bandleader's dismay.

Jazz was being stretched and molded—and so was the typical big band drumset. Ray McKinley (formerly of the Dorsey Brothers orchestra) flirted with double bass drum playing while co-leading a band with trombonist Will Bradley. The band, progressing through its boogie-woogie phase, was briefly treated to lively bottom-end phrasing and *umph*. Though the experiment didn't last long, McKinley was breaching largely uncharted territory. By employing two kicks, he showed how creative drummers were becoming.

It was inevitable that a drummer with credibility, natural talent, and celebrity status would emerge. Propelled by the gum-chewing, ever-smiling drummer Gene Krupa, The Benny Goodman Orchestra was considered one of the most technically adept, if not the most popular, recording and touring swing bands in history.

Krupa's exposure to black jazzers like Webb and white swinger Dave Tough (best known for his work with Bud Freeman and later Woody Herman), and his wild and somewhat strange stage antics, made the Chicago-born drummer the most attention-grabbing skinsman in swing.

It was as if the white and African-American jazz drumming tradition had collided in him. In Webb's chops, Krupa detected control, power, and taste—all attributes he himself would execute to the fullest. In Tough's forceful though restrained attack (Tough was almost self-deprecating and inanimate on stage, never wanting to spotlight his abilities), Krupa learned that expression and dignity could be synonymous. Ironically, Krupa would become hugely successful while being the antithesis of Tough.

Gene's flamboyant, syncopated style forced a generation, and the music world, to view drums not only as an essential instrument, but a lead one as well. Though Krupa bumped heads with clarinetist/bandleader Goodman, the drummer was a viable presence through most of Goodman's memorable moments of the 1930s. When Goodman confined himself to a small band format (which included Krupa, Goodman, vibraphonist Lionel Hampton, and pianist Teddy Wilson), Krupa knew instinctively to take his hand off the spigot: The propulsive rhythmic flow he supplied for big bands was not always necessary.

One of the most thrilling summits in musical history was a showdown involving two monolithic drum talents: Krupa and Webb. In May 1937, the Savoy in Harlem was bursting at the seams with a capacity-plus crowd. The Benny Goodman and Chick Webb orchestras were going head to head in a band battle: "Cutting sessions" were typical of the time. When word spread of what was going down at the Savoy, people flooded the area. Management had to turn people away. How many people were denied access

**Buddy Rich: "The World's Greatest Drummer"**

ing: Rich's mind-boggling ability to play nearly everything he wanted, which included a newer free-form style of jazz that was emerging, was nearly inhuman. Rich had begun playing on stage before his second birthday, and in 1939 he won the drum chair with Artie Shaw. It was a prime spot for any drummer, and it gave Rich a launching pad. It wouldn't last long, however. Despite having a bona fide hit in "Begin The Beguine," Shaw up and left during the middle of a show and vanished. (He turned up some time later south of the border.) Though the band tried to carry on without Shaw, Buddy decided to look for new employment. By the end of 1939, Rich had flipped to rival Tommy Dorsey, who was prospering from an incredible string of hits at that time. (Dorsey even had a top-ten hit LP in 1947 after the band had *dissolved*).

Besides the power supplied by Buddy Rich, Dorsey was given an added jolt of energy when he coaxed the young, sure-to-be Hollywood-bound, Hoboken-born crooner Frank Sinatra to join his band. (Sinatra had quit singing for Harry James. James, ironically, had himself recently quit Goodman's band.) Even after Sinatra left, however, the band still had a major attraction in Rich, who on occasion doubled as a dancer. Cats who didn't even like Shaw's and Tommy Dorsey's big band music would camp out at a venue just to hear, see, and feel the drummer's unbelievable command of the instrument.

Buddy urged the band to play off the written page, and over time he endeared himself to everyone he worked with—some of whom were initially turned off, or confused, by Rich's brash, constant swing assault. It was thought by many at the time (and today) that Buddy was the greatest technical, and perhaps even conceptual, drummer who ever lived. He had speed, accuracy, instincts, a superior timekeeping ability…he had it *all*.

to witness Webb and the abominable showman Krupa duking it out with triplets, rolls, and drags, we may never know.

One thing was for sure: Webb was ready to blow the roof off the place—and did—and Krupa was forever amazed and humbled by his idol's performance. The press coverage of the day gave the edge to Webb. And why not? Webb's band was sharp, up for the performance (it was on its home turf), and had done mortal combat with the normally cool/surprisingly fiery Ellington (with Sonny Greer on drums). Though Webb's orchestra would later confront Count Basie (with cool-handed rhythmatist and hi-hat master Jo Jones), it's the Goodman event that is best remembered today.

As the '30s came to a close, however, Webb, who suffered from congenital tuberculosis of the spine, succumbed to his illness. And Krupa would soon to be eclipsed by friend and technical superior Buddy Rich, dubbed "the world's greatest drummer."

It was one of the rare truths of music advertis-

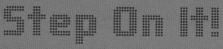

## Step On It!

As ragtime and Dixieland began to include improvisation, drummers needed to be fast and accurate just to communicate with their bandmates. Sensing this need, and frustrated by the lack of response his wooden bass drum pedal gave him, German immigrant and Chicago resident William Ludwig (of the soon-to-be famous drum company) devised a prototype metal kick pedal. Until that point, the most efficient way for a drummer to play the kick and snare simultaneously was to use his *hands*.

# The New Breed

Just around the corner, change was coming fast. Small-band jazz began to precipitate.

"Dizzy" Gillespie and Charlie "Bird" Parker were injecting an unprecedented improvisation in the music they made together, lacing it with "blue notes" (pitches in between scale tones). This new sound, dubbed "bop" or "bebop" (Benny Goodman's guitarist Charlie Christian was said to have originated the term), had the jazz establishment scratching its collective head. Younger musicians dug it, however, and bop became a growing force. Drummers like Art Blakey, Philly Joe Jones, Jimmy Cobb, and Max Roach were the rhythmic voice of a young, exploratory, and interactive jazz generation.

Soon it became clear: these bop giants were a few steps aside from the great big band drummers. Drummers—particularly Kenny Clarke—had been developing and popularizing the technique known as "dropping bombs" (shocking, timed accents on the bass drum), signaling a more interactive approach to the music. The days of big band ballads, sparkling melodies, show-off-manship, and making people dance were waning. A new age of individualism and personal expression in jazz had dawned.

A shortage of materials (all resources for making records were diverted to the war effort), a recording ban administered by the American Federation of Musicians, and Glenn Miller's disappearance in 1944 acted like the hand of fate squeezing the big band sound out of vogue. Some musicians adapted (1959's *Rich Versus Roach* is an intriguing old guard/new guard talent summit), some *tried* to jump into the flow of this new musical wave (notably Krupa), and others were completely frustrated (such as the tortured Dave Tough, who didn't live to see the end of the 1940s).

Big band would see a kind of mainstream Renaissance, however, and its magic would be spun, rediscovered, and appreciated by an unlikely generation of young, neo-hipsters during the 1990s. The beat goes on.

Art Blakey (left) and Elvin Jones bear witness to Jo Jones' singular swing.

C. Stewart

Paul Jonason

"BASIE USED TO SAY THAT THE DRUMMER IS IN THE DRIVER'S SEAT. YOU'VE GOT HOLD OF THE WHEEL, AND YOU'VE GOT TO LET THE BAND KNOW YOU'RE IN CONTROL."
—LOUIE BELLSON

# JAZZ

by
Jeff
Potter

modern jazz

Tom Copi

Old And New Dreams: Don Cherry, Dewey Redman, Charlie Haden, and Ed Blackwell

# Bebop

Not since Louis Armstrong had there been such a seismic shift. The birth of bebop marked the most influential turning point shaping the future of jazz. For drummers, it was the day of liberation.

In the early '40s, experimental jam sessions bred the foundations of the new sound. The hotbed was New York nightclub Minton's Playhouse, where spearheads such as the iconic alto saxophonist Charlie "Bird" Parker, trumpeter Dizzy Gillespie, and pianist Thelonious Monk jammed with seminal drumming giants Kenny Clarke and Max Roach.

The future now favored small bands. The emerging music was densely complex, featuring rapid, oddly phrased soloing and harmonic sophistication. In bebop, "sing-able" melody no longer reigned. Soloing and band interplay were central. In essence, jazz was no longer a popular dance music, but a listening art form.

**KENNY CLARKE AND MAX ROACH BROKE GROUND AS BOP ARCHITECTS, SCULPTING THE FUTURE OF JAZZ DRUMMING. DRUMMERS WERE FINALLY EQUAL PARTNERS.**

**Max Roach**

Clarke and Roach broke ground as bop architects, sculpting the future of jazz drumming. Drummers were finally equal partners. The ride cymbal was central to the pulse, while all four limbs became increasingly independent, free to actively accent the soloist and contribute to thematic activity. The bass drum, liberated earlier by Jo Jones from its "downbeat" role, was now fully independent along with the rest of the kit. The volcanic Art Blakey joined the front lines, introducing a trademark thick, aggressive drum surge that graced hundreds of classic tracks.

By the mid-'40s, bop was in full flower on New York's 52nd Street—"Swing Street," where devotees club-hopped, catching the cutting edge. Stan Levey backed Bird and Dizzy, and his crisp chops kept him in constant demand in the clubs and studios, eventually logging over 2,000 recordings.

Some traditionalists had balked at bop. But its influence on other styles was now undeniable. Experimenting with formats, Dizzy later applied bop to a big band, helmed by Kenny Clarke. And Woody Herman's "Second Herd" big band was given a bop infusion by the versatile Don Lamond.

Although bebop has frequently been called a revolution, that label implies a rejection of the past. In truth, the bop drummers wholly embraced their forerunners and extended their path. Their brilliance was foremost an achievement of imagination, dreaming, and reinventing what the role of the drummer could be.

The irrepressible Art Blakey. "Buhainia"'s Jazz Messengers band was a launching pad for dozens of jazz stars. And his press roll could make you cry.

Tom Copi

# The Ride Cymbal

## THE JAZZ DRUMMER'S SONIC SOUL MATE

The intimate relationship between a jazz drummer and his ride cymbal is unique. Think about it. How does a sizable disc, comprised of mysteriously concocted metals that are heated, shaped, and hammered, become such a valued friend?

Why does the jazz drummer seem to be on the eternal quest to discover "the cymbal" that will be his sonic soul mate?

The ride cymbal symbolizes the voice of the drummer in a jazz conversation. The sound created by the drumstick tip striking the surface of the cymbal is a vital link to the celebration. This sound, combined with the feeling generated by the drummer playing even beats in succession, is what inspires swing. This deceptively simple act is full of mystique. This mystique is the force that draws the jazz drummer back for further fun-filled exploration.

Have you hugged your ride cymbal today?

**Matt Wilson**

Alex Solca

# The '50s Melting Pot

Musicians hungrily assimilated and expanded upon bop's innovations, making the '50s a vibrant period of fertile cross-pollination. Bop's latter chapters boasted the exquisite Clifford Brown-Max Roach Quintet, a unit with more melodious leanings. Art Blakey formed The Jazz Messengers, the quintessential unit of "hard bop," a sound featuring a heavier, driving style with a soulful bluesy undercurrent. Blakey's unit was destined to be a long-term classic jazz institution that launched many young lions to future greatness.

An emerging giant with a modernist edge, the adventurous Roy Haynes caused a stir with archetypal bop pianist Bud Powell, then later accompanied Bird's latter years, followed by a tenure with Monk.

Parker's gifted young sideman, trumpeter Miles Davis, restlessly sought new sounds. Inspired by Gil Evans' arrangements, Miles sought to apply such rich large band textures to small groups. In 1949 and 1950, Miles cut twelve sides (later to be compiled on LP as *Birth Of*

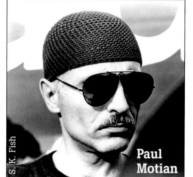

S. K. Fish

**Paul Motian**

*The Cool*), introducing new arranging horizons. Miles' nonet offered rich textures, a subtler delivery, and a focus on a more "orchestrated" ensemble sound. Again, Kenny Clarke and Max Roach held front-row seats to history. Public reception was tentative, but the long-term effect was significant.

Straining to compartmentalize the melting pot, journalists coined confounding labels like cool jazz, referring to artists such as baritone saxophonist Gerry Mulligan and trumpeter Chet Baker, whose subtler sound and gentler tones drew from the Miles sessions. The two teamed up for an influential piano-less quartet propelled by the smooth, commanding swing of Chico Hamilton.

Even more nebulous was the label "West Coast," referring to a similar sound emanating from LA. Drummers responded with a precise, nimble touch and a very "melodic" soloing approach, as represent-

Chuck Stewart

**The always sensitive Shelly Manne, shown here with noted bassist Eddie Gomez and keyboard genius Bill Evans**

Philly Joe Jones combined rudimental technique with a hard swinging style.

**"ONE CRITIC SAID, 'ROY HAYNES HAS A SMALL BASS DRUM BECAUSE HE'S A SMALL GUY.' THAT'S SO RIDICULOUS. I GOT THE SMALL DRUMS BECAUSE I HAD A SPORTS CAR, AND THEY FIT IN THE TRUNK!"**
**—ROY HAYNES**

ed by the sensitive touch of Joe Morello, the tasteful musicality of Shelly Manne (a New Yorker who cut his teeth on 52nd Street), and the elegant chamber-like work of Connie Kay with The Modern Jazz Quartet. Expanding the chamber group concept was Chico Hamilton, leading a popular a group that included cello.

Sensitive touch and musical phrasing also triumphed in Paul Motian's landmark work with pianist Bill Evans' trio. Motian "broke up" the ride cymbal patterns with an "implied" pulse and breathed with open space and elastic phrasing.

Big bands managing to evolve beyond the dance band format still found a voice in the new decade. The advent of the LP allowed Duke Ellington to expand into large-scale suites. He also revitalized his hard-swinging side with the high-energy thrust of Sam Woodyard. Stan Kenton further pursued his orchestral approach, at one point flirting with a thirty-nine-piece ensemble anchored by Shelly Manne.

Drawing from hard bop, other drummers were employing a more modern, hard-swinging, and less angular "straight-ahead" sound that earned them a prolific recording output. Examples include the popping propulsion of Art Taylor, as heard on many Prestige recordings and later with saxophonist John Coltrane on *Giant Steps*...Philly Joe Jones' marvelous command with Miles' classic quintet of 1955-58 and on countless Blue Note releases...and the tasteful economical swing of Jimmy Cobb, as heard in his years with Miles' band and pianist Wynton Kelly's trio.

Again, Miles bookended the decade with an influential style shift. Maintaining his restrained, cooler sound, he released *Kind Of Blue*, heralding "modal jazz," a concept based upon soloing on modes and scales rather than chords. Jimmy Cobb complemented the wide-open feel of the new palette with his swinging "easy" feel and judicious use of space. A far more radical signpost was the New York arrival of composer/alto saxophonist Ornette Coleman, whose initial releases hinted at the turbulence of the decade ahead.

Tom Copi

# Rim Shots

## DRUMS IN THE MOVIES

by Will Romano

The drum might have been man's first instrument, but strangely enough, they've never gotten much play on the big screen. In Hollywood, drums are more often famously used in reference to war and life-threatening disease than to music. (See *Drums Along The Mohawk*, 1913's silent-era Civil War short *Drummer Of The Eighth*, and *Bang The Drum Slowly*.)

Thankfully, a number of daring filmmakers over the years have broken with tradition and incorporated drums and drummers into their more musical celluloid dreams. One of the most popular drum movies of all time is 1959's *The Gene Krupa Story*, which explores the legendary swing drummer's many loves and addictions—sometimes flip sides of the same coin.

Sal Mineo, best known for his role as Plato in *Rebel Without A Cause*, is at home playing troubled individuals, and *The Gene Krupa Story* is no exception. Krupa had his share of ups and downs, but on the whole the film is generally uptempo. In a particularly inspiring scene involving Krupa's return to the spotlight after run-ins with the law (i.e., drug problems), Krupa wins over a vocal and hostile crowd with the help of friend Dave Tough, played by real-life drum hero Shelly Manne. (The film,

released as *Drum Crazy* in the UK, was so inspiring that a young Keith Moon knew upon his first viewing what he wanted to do for the rest of his life.) Though Krupa recorded the drum performances himself for the film, Mineo was something more than a drum hobbyist, as his convincing stick control bears out. The actor expertly recalls Krupa's slouched posture, over-the-top showmanship, and goonish facial expressions.

In *The Man With The Golden Arm*, Frank Sinatra portrays once-strung-out ex-con poker dealer Frankie Machine, who's starting life over clean and off the junk. Frankie dreams of being a professional drummer, but this career path doesn't come easy to him. Inevitably, Frankie slides back into a life of card shufflin' and substance abuse when his confidence as a drummer sags. A powerful film well worth the price of admission. (Sinatra is believable as a tortured soul, and Darren McGavin is great as the devilish, conniving drug peddler.) Check out The Chairman practicing and running brushes over a snare head.

In 1970s anachronistic musical/western/comedy *Zachariah*, jazz icon Elvin Jones is Job Cain, a gunslinging baaaad-ass quick-draw with a $50,000 bounty on his head. In the wacky spirit of the film, Elvin finishes a gunfight the victor, then kicks Jim Fox (of the real-life band The James Gang) off his kit to make some more

banging noises—with drums, not a pistol. (Didn't every high-profile outlaw in the Old West take a time out to play a drum solo every now and then?)

Other drummers have found themselves on the business end of a camera, such as Ringo Starr, Phil Collins (he had a bit part in *A Hard Day's Night* and starred in other films), Sheila E., Miguel Ferrer (who was a drummer before his acting career took off), Buddy Rich, and Keith Moon, who's in such movies as *Tommy* (as Uncle Ernie), *Sextette* (with Mae West), *That'll Be The Day*, *Stardust*, and Frank Zappa's *200 Motels*.

Movies to rent: *The Doors*, *This Is Spinal Tap!* (saying drummers run a streak of bad luck in this one is an understatement), *'Round Midnight*, *Help!*, *Birth*

*Of The Beatles*, *Backbeat*, *The Commitments*, *Mo' Better Blues*, the holiday TV classic *The Little Drummer Boy*, *Some Kind Of Wonderful* (drummin' tomboy Mary Stuart Masterson pines for a clueless Eric Stoltz), *Nothing In Common* (with Tom Hanks, Jackie Gleason, and Sela Ward), *The Song Remains The Same*, *Singles*, *That Thing You Do!*, and 2002's *Drumline*, a flick about a southern university drum team, with some amazing choreographed drumming.

# The Explosive '60s

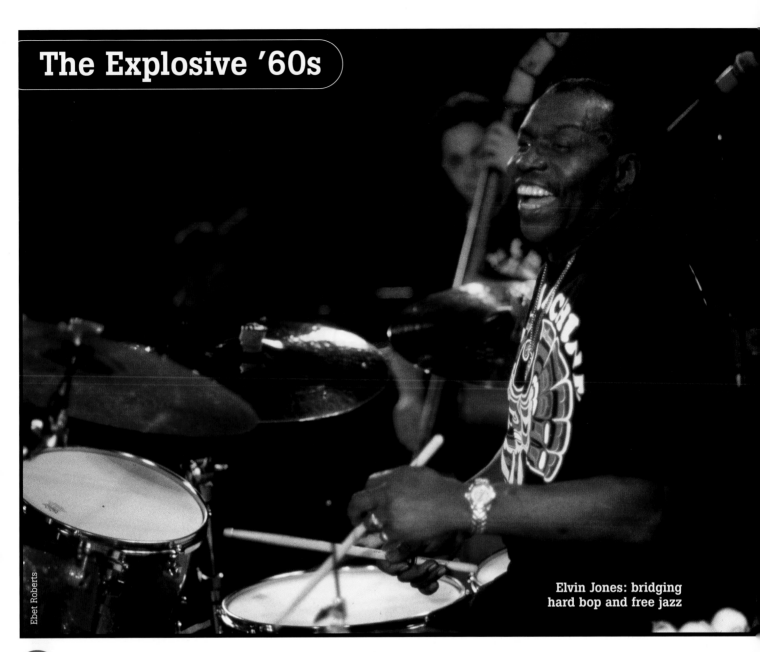

Ebet Roberts

**Elvin Jones: bridging hard bop and free jazz**

The seeds of "free jazz" were planted. Ornette's playing showed a rhythmically elastic linear expression not strictly bound to chord changes. Ed Blackwell and Billy Higgins, versatile drummers with roots in R&B as well as traditional jazz, responded with a similar open-minded spontaneity. Higgins graduated to be one of the most recorded jazz drummers of the next decade, in demand for his tasteful and "loose" yet driving time feel. Coleman's influence was strong, and so was the controversy.

The '60s were marked by experimentation and a liberal atmosphere, allowing for the traditional to coexist with the avant-garde. Dannie Richmond combined "free" influences and earthy swing and bluesy feels within the complex structures of bassist Charles Mingus's music. Never content to coast, bop Godfather Max Roach released *Drums Unlimited,* featuring drum solos as pieces in themselves. As his art become increasingly political, Max delivered messages of civil rights in such ambitious works as

*Freedom Now Suite.*

On the opposite pole to the jolting free school, many star pianists enjoyed success by favoring lyricism. These popular leaders brought out the best in sensitive "melodic" drumming, as represented by Denzil Best's infectious brushwork with George Shearing and Erroll Garner, Ed Thigpen's masterly brushwork with dynamo Oscar Peterson, and Joe Morello's experiments with odd time signatures as a member of The Dave Brubeck Quartet. Monk found ideal complements for his quirky colorful invention with drummers Ben Riley and Frankie Dunlop.

Vital drummer-led big bands appeared. Super-drummer Buddy Rich formed a big band in '66 that proved to be a lengthy and great success. In '65, Mel Lewis co-formed the influential Thad Jones-Mel Lewis Orchestra, a long-lived institution of greats. Lewis proved that a subtle, solid swing could wield authority without bombast. After heightening his polyrhythmic sound with

Tony Williams led the transition from mainstream
swing to freer styles, and ultimately to fusion.

# THE '60S WERE MARKED BY EXPERIMENTATION AND A LIBERAL ATMOSPHERE, ALLOWING FOR THE TRADITIONAL TO COEXIST WITH THE AVANT-GARDE.

saxophonists John Coltrane and Stan Getz, Roy Haynes finally came into his own as a leader.

It was an explosive decade of boundary stretching. But the towering innovative turning point belonged to Elvin Jones. The mighty big-grinned drummer artfully bridged the aggressive hard bop of the Blakey school and the new "free" influences. Elvin's concept reached fruition in his years with the epic John Coltrane Quartet, peaking with *A Love Supreme* (1964). Elvin embraced Coltrane's spiritual cascading modal improvisations with waves of rhythms. His overlapped rhythmic layers, or "polyrhythms," were dense, fluid, and loud. The drums' presence was intrinsic, not a "backing." Elvin's pulse was a holistic sonic surge, rather than a linear definition. In whole, it was a cathartic outpouring that changed drumset expression forever.

Another major catalyst was Tony Williams. In 1963, while he was still in his teens, Tony was recruited by Miles. During his six-year tenure, the prodigy contributed to one of Miles' most progressive quintets, scoring a string of groundbreaking LPs. Tony's fleet, razor-sharp cymbal ride was jaw-dropping, his interweaving polyrhythms precise and defined. His interplay with soloists was downright clairvoyant. Most of all, Tony managed to "break up" and displace patterns, accents, and subdivisions without sacrificing an urgent driving momentum. Also a constant presence on Blue Note recordings, Williams cut classics with artists such as pianist Herbie Hancock and reedman Eric Dolphy, whose *Out To Lunch* allowed the drummer to stretch his "open" style even further. In '69, The Tony Williams Lifetime debuted, foreshadowing '70s jazz-fusion.

Billy Higgins was one of the most recorded drummers of the modern era.

Clayton Call

# FREE JAZZ

Rashied Ali with John Coltrane, Han Bennink with any number of improvisational giants. Since the early '60s, the concept of "free" drumming—where even meter is subtracted from the equation, leaving a blank canvas of sound and time—has intrigued and enraged drummers across the stylistic spectrum. "The drummer's job is to keep time!" exclaims drummer number 1. "But why?" demands drummer number 2. "Aren't all means of expression valid?" Clearly, in the right hands, in the right circumstances, free drumming *can* be musical. Often it's not. Perhaps the important point is that the door to freedom *was* once boldly opened by our drumming forefathers, even if most of us prefer to remain on this side of it.

"WE NEED A CERTAIN AMOUNT OF DISCIPLINE IN ORDER TO UNDERSTAND WHAT IT IS TO BE OPEN AND FREE. IF YOU DON'T KNOW WHAT DISCIPLINE IS, YOU DON'T KNOW WHAT FREEDOM IS EITHER."

—ELVIN JONES

Joost Leijen

by Robin Tolleson

R&B master Fred Below

As a member of Motown's house band, The Funk Brothers, drummer Richard "Pistol" Allen played on countless hit songs.

Leni Sinclair

The urbanization of America around the time of the Second World War had unforeseen but immense musical consequences. As job seekers moved to industrial cities like New York, Detroit, Chicago, Memphis, Philadelphia, and Oakland, a new musical genre sprang up. It was a mix of the southern blues, boogie woogie, and the pop of the day, as performed by Louis Jordan and Charles Brown. It didn't really have a name that stuck until 1949, when the music trade magazine *Billboard* changed the name of its "race records" chart to "rhythm & blues." Names like Hank Ballard, Chubby Checker, The Coasters, and Bobby Bland frequented the Top-10 and helped define the music.

There were new demands on drummers as R&B took hold. Now a drummer had to be able to play a red-hot two-beat Gospel stomp, a bluesy backbeat shuffle (Bernard Purdie's trademark), a refined, in-the-pocket 12/8 ballad, and a hybrid of all the above, like the groove Earl Palmer left on Fats Domino's "Walkin' To New Orleans."

Drummers up to the task in the early days of R&B included Charlie Persip with Ray Charles, Earl Phillips with Howlin' Wolf and others on the Chess label, Fred Below with Chuck Berry, and Sam Lay with Paul Butterfield. These drummers and many others paved the way for soul drummers of the early 1960s like Panama Francis (Ray Charles's "Drowning In My Own Tears"), Idris Muhammad (Fats Domino, Roberta Flack, Sam Cooke, Jerry Butler),

## A DRUMMER NOW HAD TO BE ABLE TO PLAY A RED-HOT TWO-BEAT GOSPEL STOMP, A BLUESY BACKBEAT SHUFFLE, A REFINED, IN-THE-POCKET 12/8 BALLAD—AND A HYBRID OF ALL THE ABOVE.

Marvin Gaye (a house drummer at Motown before becoming a superstar vocalist), Morris Jennings, (Donny Hathaway, Curtis Mayfield), and the above-mentioned Bernard Purdie (James Brown, Aretha Franklin, King Curtis) and Earl Palmer (Little Richard, Four Tops, Smokey Robinson).

The soul era saw a rise in "message music," in a mix of fat down-tempo grooves and stirring double-time hand-clappers.

Booker T. & The MG's, featuring backbeat master Al Jackson Jr. (right). As the house band for Hi and Stax Records, The MG's played on nearly every major hit to come out of Memphis in the '60s.

Session great Earl Palmer combined a New Orleans feel with a solid R&B groove. Like later studio star Steve Gadd, Palmer developed his rhythmic sense early in life as a tap dancer.

Lissa Wales

Born out of racially tense times, soul took rotation spots from the sometime saccharine R&B of the day on the AM airwaves, starting around 1964. Soul music combined the feel of Gospel with lyrics that were often quite earthy. The grittiness of the drums was coming through on recordings now too. Rhythm "sections" began to establish themselves in major recording cities, and certain drummers stood out.

Al Jackson Jr. and Sammy Creason were the top drummers in the 1960s Memphis scene, playing with Stax and Volt stars such as Al Green, Wilson Pickett, Sam & Dave, and Isaac Hayes. Jackson, who was also part of Booker T. & The MG's, had a knack for making difficult parts sound simple. Check out Al Green's "I'm Still In Love With You"—a slow soul groove percolated with a slightly swinging hip-hop-ish hi-hat lick, an inventive back-and-forth between a snare hit and low-tom bomb on "2," and cross-stick on "4." Jackson had one of the most relaxed pockets in the biz, but on Green's "Love And Happiness" he's insistent, pumping incessantly with the occasional hi-hat chirp and snare double backbeat.

William "Benny" Benjamin, Uriel Jones, and Richard "Pistol" Allen were part of Motown's Funk Brothers rhythm section, along with Eddie "Bongo" Brown and tambourine expert Jack Ashford. They played on countless hits out of Motor City by The Supremes, The Temptations, Martha Reeves & The Vandellas, and many others.

Atlantic Records always surrounded its top soul stars Aretha Franklin and Ray Charles with great bands, including the most solid, purposeful drummers. Charles' Atlantic compilation *The Birth Of Soul* features drummers Connie Kay, Alonzo Stewart, Oscar Moore, Panama Francis, Glenn Brooks, and William Peebles. Aretha's *Queen Of Soul: The Atlantic Recordings* features Bernard Purdie, Ray Lucas, Roger Hawkins, Quinton Joseph, Sammy Creason, Rick Marotta, Ed Greene, and Bruno Carr. Purdie shows his versatility on Aretha's *Live At Fillmore West*, with a high-octane Gospel version of "Respect," a commanding, reverential backbeat on "Bridge Over Troubled Water," and playful 16th-note kick punches on "Eleanor Rigby."

Meanwhile, drummer Ron Tutt gave Elvis Presley's "In The Ghetto" a strong soul feel, and drummer Floyd Sneed was the rhythmic powerhouse behind the blue-eyed soul trio Three Dog Night. (Check out Sneed's syncopated groove on their hit "Black & White.") James Gadson's strong playing propelled Charles Wright & The Watts 103rd Street Rhythm Band ("Express Yourself"). And the work of James Brown's early drummers—like Nate Jones, William Bowman, Clayton Fillyau, Melvin Parker, Nat Kendrick, and Obie Williams—set the stage for the funk era to come.

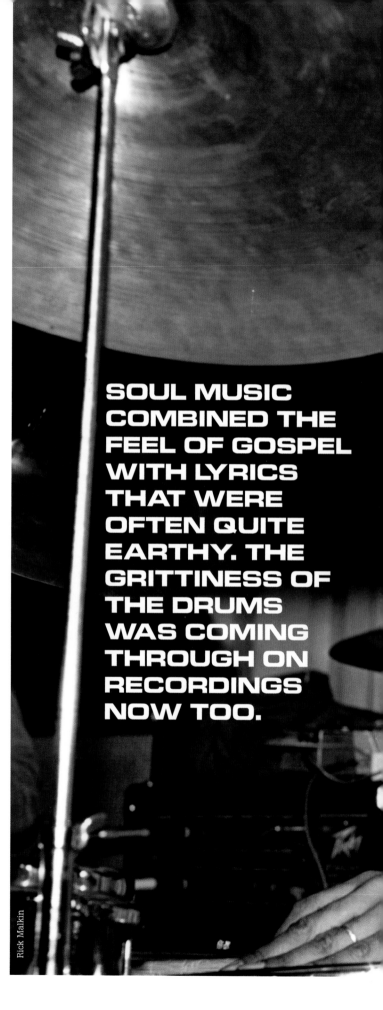

SOUL MUSIC COMBINED THE FEEL OF GOSPEL WITH LYRICS THAT WERE OFTEN QUITE EARTHY. THE GRITTINESS OF THE DRUMS WAS COMING THROUGH ON RECORDINGS NOW TOO.

Rick Malkin

Idris Muhammad works successfully in the jazz and R&B worlds, a rare achievement indeed.

Cream's Ginger Baker, rock's first great drum soloist, was also an early pioneer of world music, via his own large bands and collaborations with Afrobeat great Fela Kuti.

# ROCK

by Adam Budofsky

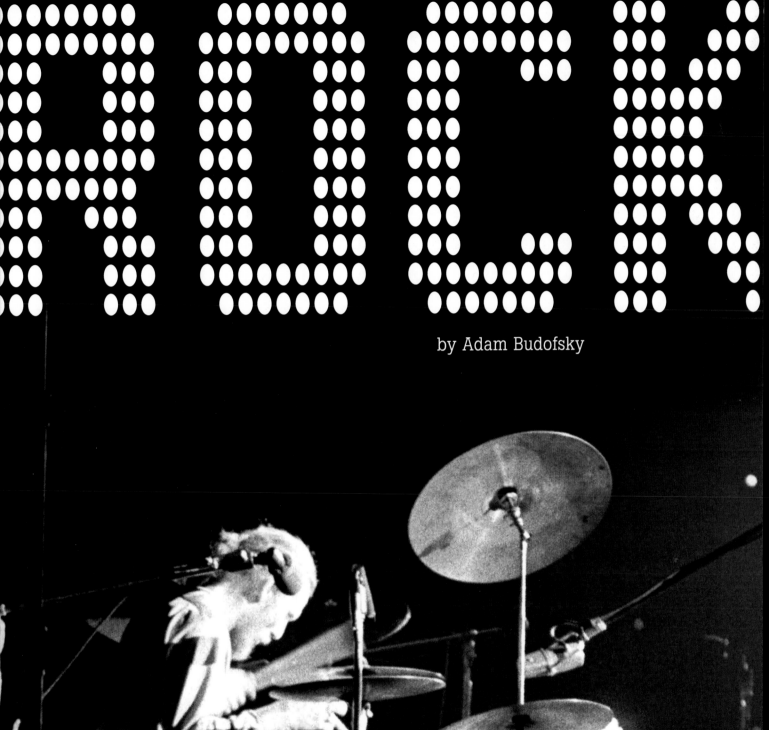

# There was rock 'n' roll.
# Then there was **rock.**

In the early '60s, Western society was on the verge of severe upheaval. Politics, family, religion, education, race, gender—everything was changing. In America, black R&B musicians were redefining popular music, combining sophisticated melodic ideas with killer dance floor beats. In England, teenagers were discovering these hip sounds, as well as more "old-fashioned" blues records, which they found mysterious and exotic. In response to the very new world they found themselves in, the post-war generation imagined the possibilities of these American styles, and rearranged them in their own image.

Today we call this era "classic rock," as if it were created by wise old men with a desire to preserve the past. Nothing could be further from the truth (at least not at first). The earliest and best classic rock bands were living in the now, making music as big and freaky as they could. The drummers lucky enough to find themselves working in these tumultuous times needed to invent their own styles within the changing landscape, and the best of these musicians helped draw a blueprint for rock music that's still being followed today.

From left: Ringo Starr with The Beatles, The Who's Keith Moon, and Mitch Mitchell of The Jimi Hendrix Experience

**B**ack in England, young players on the cutting edge were grooving to American soul at night, and hunting down import blues recordings by day. Chuck Berry, Muddy Waters, John Lee Hooker, Howlin' Wolf...these men were considered *gods* to young British musicians, even as they were being largely ignored in their homeland. Americans paid for neglecting their own national treasures—at record company cash registers, where they gobbled up albums by "British Invasion" bands selling their own culture back to them, though with a modern new sheen.

Most of the great classic rock bands and singers we think of today had their roots in mid-'60s Britain. The Beatles, Led Zeppelin, The Rolling Stones, The Who, Jimi Hendrix, Fleetwood Mac, Bad Company, The Kinks, David Bowie, Traffic, The Faces, Deep Purple, Rod Stewart, and Cream either had hits during that period or featured players who were formulating their styles then.

Despite the success of Gene Krupa during the big band days, before the mid-'60s, most drummers in pop situations were still expected to politely smile while the singer up front handled the showmanship. But these were different times. Bigger rooms demanded more drama onstage, and the trend toward artists performing their own material broke the doors wide open for bands to set themselves apart by focusing on individual musicianship. The drummer was not only allowed to be a part of the show now, he was *expected* to be.

## THESE WERE DIFFERENT TIMES. THE DRUMMER WAS NOT ONLY ALLOWED TO BE A PART OF THE SHOW—HE WAS *EXPECTED* TO BE.

The Beatles are universally cited as the band that started the British music revolution. Though there were other groups in the very early '60s who shared common influences—American pop and R&B from Buddy Holly to Little Richard, as well as British "skiffle" music—The Beatles made their mark first, and loudest. Early hits like "She Loves You" and "I Want To Hold Your Hand," experienced by thousands of American teenagers for the first time during the band's historic performances on the *Ed Sullivan* TV variety show in 1964, helped fuel Beatlemania, a pop culture frenzy that obliterated nearly every other movement of the time. The number of future musicians who refer to those shows as the beginning of their

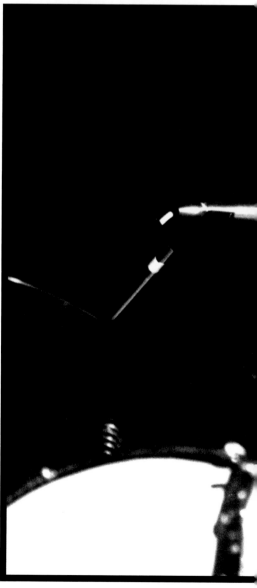

This page, clockwise from top left: Mick Fleetwood of Fleetwood Mac, Dino Danelli of The Rascals, Charlie Watts of The Rolling Stones, Bev Bevan of The Electric Light Orchestra. Facing page, clockwise from top right: Danny Seraphine of Chicago, Simon Kirke of Bad Co., John Densmore and The Doors, Traffic's Jim Capaldi, The Band's Levon Helm, and John Bonham of Led Zeppelin

Bob Gruen

Tom Copi

Edward Przydzial/ECPI-Archives

Starfile

Tom Copi

obsession with rock 'n' roll is incalculable. And Ringo Starr, perched on the drum riser at his Ludwig kit, head cocked, smile permanently fixed, hair bobbing and hands slapping, immediately became *the* most influential drummer of the age—and perhaps of all time.

With any cultural phenomenon, a backlash inevitably begins, and there have certainly been plenty of "schooled" musicians (and just plain ignorant folks) who've denigrated Ringo for a lack of technique. Those who were truly listening, though, knew this was balderdash. First of all, Paul McCartney and John Lennon were the greatest songwriters of their generation, and they had no reason to stick with a sub-par drummer. Further, Ringo had such a natural swing and sway, it was easy to miss the finer points, including his fast hands, feel for song dynamics, ability to come up with unique but appropriate parts, and knack for supporting the myriad styles that Lennon, McCartney, and lead guitarist George Harrison threw at him.

As The Beatles' music became more sophisticated with each new record, Ringo's style adapted and progressed. From his powerful engineering of early hits like "Help," to his chamber-pop orchestrations on *Rubber Soul*, to the psychedelic rumblings on "Rain" and "Tomorrow Never Knows," Ringo consistently came up with the perfect complement to perfect pop songs.

By 1967/68, it was all about psychedelic rock on both sides of the Atlantic. In America, the emphasis was largely on songwriting, ensemble play, and re-imagining home-grown styles like folk, country, and jazz. In LA, The Doors, featuring singer Jim Morrison and Elvin Jones fanatic John Densmore, celebrated attaining higher levels of consciousness. Morrison's beguiling lyrics were expertly accentuated by Densmore's impressionistic attacks, most notably on the cut "When The Music's Over."

Meanwhile, up in the Bay Area, Michael Schrieve—another Elvin disciple—brought rhythmic sparks to guitarist Carlos Santana's Latin blues. And John Fogerty's Credence Clearwater Revival saw Doug Clifford faking out most radio listeners with grooves that sounded like they came right out of The Bayou. In

Georgia, the Allman Brothers' dual drummer team of Butch Trucks and Jaimoe Johanson served up the greasiest tandem rhythms on FM radio.

The most "American" of the classic rock drummers is Levon Helm of The Band. The group was famous before their first album came out, largely from their collaborations with Bob Dylan during his residence in New York's Catskill mountains. The Band abetted some of Dylan's most outrageous and fruitful musical experiments, many of which were heard by the public for the first time years later on the famous *Basement Tapes* double album. Levon, the only American among a group of Canadians, was clearly an old soul, and he imbued The Band's literate and rocking Americana with a timeless feel and heartbreaking tom fills.

For many, The Band were a signal in a new direction, away from the crazed bombast of England's more severe psychedelic rock, best represented by The Jimi Hendrix Experience, featuring Mitch Mitchell, and Cream, with Ginger Baker. Mitchell used the big band pyrotechnics of Buddy Rich as a jumping-off point for his influential performances and recordings with Hendrix, who was, bar none, the flashiest and most advanced electric guitarist of the rock scene. Baker too supported a guitar god (Eric Clapton) as Cream pushed the boundaries of improvisation in rock music. Baker's performance on "Toad" is a milestone in drum soloing,

## MOON APPROACHED THE ACCENTING IT AS HE SAW INHIBITION, AND USUALLY

and his upside-down beat on "Sunshine Of Your Love" is wonderfully indicative of his unique approach.

With the possible exception of Ringo Starr, the two drummers who left the *most* enduring marks on modern rock drumming were The Who's Keith Moon and Led Zeppelin's John Bonham. Moon—who is responsible (or at least *credited*) for more episode of rock excess than any other musician in history, drummer or

**Elton John's Nigel Olsson and Queen's Roger Taylor**

Kevin Pierce

Little Feat's Richie Hayward (above) and Don Brewer of Grand Funk Railroad

otherwise—was also the most unusual and dramatic drummer ever to set foot onstage. The classic image of Moony is in concert, arms and legs flying impossibly fast in a blur of emotion and theater, spitting out seemingly random fills that match guitarist Pete Townshend's six-string caterwauling in excitement, if not always note-for-note.

The Who were the wildest and most ambitious band of their anyone had heard in 1968, when their self-titled debut hit, and Bonham was clearly a big reason for that. In fact, today, John Bonham's signature grooves are admired as *the* benchmark for heavy rock drumming. Interestingly, the secret to Bonzo's famous feel is more often than not missed by aspiring drummers, who focus on his famous solo prowess and unmistakable licks rather than his insanely deep groove.

# WHO'S MUSIC LIKE A JAZZ DRUMMER MIGHT, FIT, IN THE MOMENT, WITHOUT TO GREAT EFFECT.

time, and Moony was its center. Grinning from behind his increasingly huge Premier drumsets, forever crash-riding his cymbals (often without a hi-hat in sight), flipping double bass triplet ideas here, there, and everywhere, Keith approached the Who's music like a jazz drummer might, accenting it as he saw fit, in the moment, without inhibition, and usually to great effect.

Amazingly, Keith on record was just as devastating. His performances on *Who's Next* (1971) and *Quadrophenia* (1973), for instance, represent a perfect balance of technique and passion, within music that was as demanding and passionate as anything else being recorded at the time. Sadly, Keith Moon died in 1978 after an apparent overdose from drugs that he was taking to combat alcoholism. There's been no drummer who's touched his unique slant on rock and rhythm since.

John Bonham was a hot but relatively unrecorded up & comer when he was tapped to join guitar slinger Jimmy Page's "New Yardbirds," soon renamed Led Zeppelin following a chat and a pint with members of The Who. Zeppelin was the heaviest band

Bonham would record eight studio albums with Zeppelin before dying in his sleep following a long night of extremely heavy drinking. Those original Zeppelin records contain so much creative, slamming heavy rock drumming that many a modern player has made a career out of aping only one aspect of Bonzo's legacy. If the king of rock 'n' roll was Elvis Presley, then the king of rock drumming was certainly John Bonham.

Other British drummers who made history during classic rock's heyday include Charlie Watts with The Rolling Stones, Ian Paice with Deep Purple, Bev Bevan with The Move and later The Electric Light Orchestra, Kenney Jones with The Small Faces and The Faces, Jim Capaldi with Traffic, Mickey Waller with Jeff Beck and Rod Stewart, Mick Fleetwood with Fleetwood Mac, Simon Kirke with Free and later Bad Company, Nigel Olsson with Elton John, Roger Taylor with Queen, Tony Newman with Jeff Beck and T. Rex, Jerry Shirley with Humble Pie, Buddy Miles with Jimi Hendrix's Band Of Gypsys, Lee Kerslake with Uriah Heep, and Dennis Davis with David Bowie.

As the '70s progressed, "arena rock," with its larger-than-life riffs and big beats, turned the spotlight back on drummers from The States and Canada, where long tours playing huge "sheds" had become the norm for hit-making rock bands. Don Brewer of Grand Funk Railroad was a soloing titan who played with an unmatched sense of purpose. Danny Seraphine developed a distinct jazz-influenced rock style with Chicago, who cranked out hit after hit. Richie Hayward turned many heads with his individualistic approach to New Orleans and funk grooves with the hugely influential Little Feat. And Peter Criss, though never considered a technical powerhouse, nonetheless influenced thousands of young drummers attracted to the theatrics of KISS, who by certain measures were the biggest rock band of the decade.

By the late '70s, as punk rock and new wave became the catchwords among hip music fans, classic rock was increasingly used as a disparaging term, indicating "dinosaur" bands who'd lost their mojo, and whose influence was waning among upcoming musicians. Several bands successfully straddled the competing musical paths, notably Tom Petty & The Heartbreakers featuring Stan Lynch, Cheap Trick with Bun E. Carlos, Heart with Michael DeRosier, and Aerosmith with Joey Kramer. But it wouldn't be until the early '90s, with the arrival of grunge rock, that the early classic rock groups would again be lauded for their revolutionary contributions. The '80s would be a long, cold decade for all except the most resilient of the original classic rock bands. But those who toughed it out would live to see their early works used as the basis for a whole new generation of future rock gods.

Joey Kramer of Aerosmith

Paul Natkin

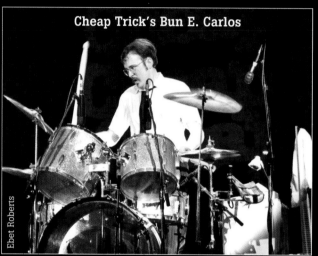

Cheap Trick's Bun E. Carlos

Ebet Roberts

# The Shaping Of A

In junior high and high school, my band rehearsed in my parents' house. First in the attic, then in the basement. Then in the attic. Then finally in the basement. Which means this was where I practiced my drumming.

I never quite learned how to *practice* per se, but I played all the time, so I got better. To my credit and perhaps in some ways my detriment I tried not to bite off too much more than I could chew. Until I reached a certain level of ability, I kept it simple. I played while blasting records and tapes through dreadful headphones—all treble and no bass; yank 'em off too quick and you'll mangle an ear.

But I had good taste. I played along with Stan Lynch of Tom Petty & The Heartbreakers, approximating his colorful fills on stuff like "Even The Losers" and "The Waiting." I did my best and certainly benefited greatly from playing along with Jeff Porcaro on Steely Dan's *Katy Lied* LP. "Doctor Wu" helped me with my tom work

and cross-sticking, and pushed me to begin developing a sense of groove. Plus it gave me an excuse to use the chimes I got for Christmas. "Rose Darling" was brisk enough to my fifteen-year-old hands that I tried to double up by hitting the ride alternately with the butt end and tip of the stick. Ah,

but soon I learned it was my *ears* that were deficient; I could use soft snare strokes called ghost notes to create what I was hearing as an extra-fast ride pattern.

Jeez, I even had the audacity to play along with my hero, John Bonham, on Led Zeppelin's *Presence* LP. (Yes, I'm among the,

Tom Petty & The Heartbreakers'
Stan Lynch

# "MOMMY, DADDY! I WANNA PLAY THE DRUMS!"

The Monkees might have been derided by "cool" kids into The Stones, The Who, and the pre-fab four's obvious template, The Beatles. But there's no denying their massive popularity, and the huge number of kids who must have caught the drumming bug after watching Micky Dolenz on TV, gleefully kicking out "I'm A Believer" and "Stepping Stone" on his impossibly bizarre drum setup. The fact that studio heavies like Hal Blaine were responsible for recording most of The Monkees' songs didn't really matter (except to give lie to accusations that their records were second-rate). What *was* important was that The Monkees were clearly having a ball. Other TV drummers who turned on legions of would-be players include *The Tonight Show*'s Ed Shaughnessy, *Late Night*'s Anton Fig, and Animal from *The Muppets*.

Courtesy of Rhino Records

# Rock Drummer
by Michael Parillo

oh, fifty or sixty percent of rock drummers who proudly and sincerely list Bonham as our primary influence.) Who knows what the hell I was playing, but it was *something*. I began to listen analytically and slow things down to figure them out. "Nobody's Fault But Mine" showed me that I had to be able to crash with my snare hand as well as my ride hand.

It's a treat to follow literally in another drummer's footsteps, to trace his or her design and feel what it's like to draw it with your own pen. It feeds your mind and gives your body new memories to build upon. Fresh ideas follow hard and fast.

Your Stan Lynch and Jeff Porcaro might've been Phil Rudd and Neil Peart. Jamie Oldaker and Alex Van Halen. Carter Beauford and Josh Freese. But you know what I mean. We're all still rocking with the drummers who inspired us in the first place. We owe these people a great debt, as we owe those who themselves gave birth to the Lynches and Porcaros and Rudds and Pearts

and therefore the mes and yous.

As I continued to develop as a drummer, whatever actual honest-to-goodness practicing I did—and sure, I did some—often happened away from the drumset. When I sat at the kit, it was too tempting just to frolic to my heart's content. If I wasn't "soloing" (read: doing whatever came out that day) or playing along with records, I was taking off my toms' bottom heads and hanging the drums at sharp angles like Phil Collins or arranging everything perfectly flat like Ginger Baker. And sometimes, in that quiet time just after a good session, with my heart beating fast and my ears ringing loud, I would sit and stare at my kit, thinking, *O, percussive array of circular objects, how I love thee*. I still do this, sometimes even nodding toward my gear during a set break to a bandmate or audience member like I'm pointing out a cute girl on the street.

So between all these important activities, there wasn't much time to really buckle down in my drum room and work on rudi-

ments and stuff like that. But I had an even better time for practicing: while sitting in class. When I told Mr. Sheehan I had really learned a lot in his algebra seminar, I wasn't talking about vectors and coefficients—I was talking about double strokes and paradiddles. What a sweet deal we drummers have. We can work on our stickings without sticks; we can surreptitiously develop hand-foot patterns when no one's looking, or even when someone *is* looking! And we can do these things, play these figures that we will soon perform at earsplitting volumes, *quietly*.

We may have to lug more gear than our bandmates, not to mention having to essentially build our instrument every time we move it (and then having to tear it down again), but it's well worth it: We get to play the drums. Whether we're self-taught punkers, highly schooled fusion freaks, or anything in between, we are part of a special club. It's an honor to be a drummer.

# THE JOURN

by Adam Budofsky

Despite what music encyclopedias and awards ceremonies would lead us to believe, the history of rock 'n' roll is largely written by musicians who aren't household names, and who aren't affiliated with just one singer, band, or even style.

These players—the journeymen, let's call them—make a career in the studios and on tour by expertly reading a musical situation, providing what's needed, and when the time is right, moving on to the next gig.

Often these players aren't lavished with the same kind of praise and attention long-time bandmembers receive. But that doesn't always reflect the reality of their contributions. In fact, journeymen drummers are responsible for some of the most familiar and imitated drum performances in history.

Randy Bachman

Quintessential journeyman drummer Aynsley Dunbar. Many classic rock bands benefitted from his presence.

Carmine Appice is perhaps the most notable journey-man drummer in rock 'n' roll. Appice first came to prominence with The Vanilla Fudge, a psychedelic rock band from Long Island, New York, who floored people in 1967 with their bombastic approach to covers such as "You Keep Me Hangin' On," originally by Motown's Supremes. Carmine, who can fairly lay claim to having influenced future rock gods like Led Zeppelin's John Bonham, has always been an extroverted player unafraid to call attention to the drum riser. He's backed up his larger-than-life image with dramatic chops and a deep feel, which he used to great effect in the ensuing years with heavy rock supergroup Beck, Bogert & Appice, and with Rod Stewart, with whom he co-wrote the smash hit "Do Ya Think I'm Sexy." Carmine was also one of the first rock drummers to put out a successful instructional book and perform wide-scale drum clinics. He still regularly records and tours, including his recent band with guitar slinger Pat Travers.

The late, great Cozy Powell was one of the most beloved drummers to come out of England in the mid-'60s. Powell could be relied on to add a rock-solid rhyth-mic bed to any hard-rock scenario, and his slamming beat and thunderous hand-foot combinations can be heard on dozens of albums with people like Black Sabbath, Jeff Beck, Whitesnake, Robert Plant, The Michael Schenker Group, and especially Rainbow. Check out Cozy's intro to their epic cut "Stargazer" for a taste of his classic output.

Like many a British classic-rock star, including Eric Clapton, Mick Fleetwood, and The Stones' Mick Taylor, Aynsley Dunbar came out of John Mayall's Bluesbreakers, a virtual blues-rock finishing school. Besides leading his own band, Dunbar contributed to important LPs by Jeff Beck, Frank Zappa, David Bowie, John Lennon, Lou Reed, Journey, Jefferson Starship, and Whitesnake.

Hunt Sales, the drum-playing son of legendary comedi-an Soupy Sales, can be heard on television nearly every night; it's his killer take on the "Can't Hurry Love" Motown beat that powers Iggy Pop's timeless cut "Lust For Life," which has been used as the music behind TV commercial campaigns as often as any other song in recent history. The other half of Iggy's rhythm section was Hunt's brother, bassist Tony Sales, who also worked with the drummer in David Bowie's scorching early-'90s band Tin Machine. Drummers who were floored by Bowie's smoking, adventurous rhythmatist with the over-sized drums might have done a little research and found that Hunt initially came to prominence with '70s super-

Tommy Aldridge

Bill Crump

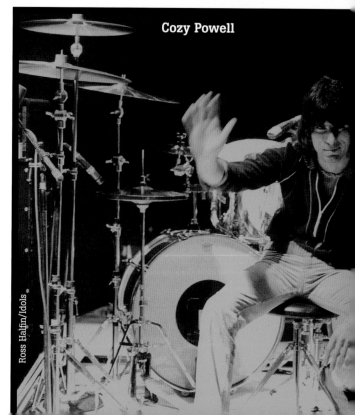

Cozy Powell

Ross Halfin/idols

star Todd Rundgren—at the age of *fourteen*.

Tommy Aldridge made his name as the fiery solo maestro with Southern rock burners Black Oak Arkansas ("Jim Dandy To The Rescue"). Aldridge later left a permanent impression on the music

Carmine Appice

Rick Malkin

of Ozzy Osbourne, Gary Moore, Whitesnake, Thin Lizzy, and Ted Nugent, and is still revered for his ability to dependably bring the rock to any recording or touring situation.

Other journeymen rock drummers who've laid down some serious tracks—and serious air mileage—include Prairie Prince (The Tubes, Jefferson Starship, Todd Rundgren, Chris Isaak, Brian Eno & David Byrne, XTC), Gregg Bissonette (Gino Vanelli, David Lee Roth, Toto, Don Henley, Duran Duran), Denny Carmassi (Montrose, Heart, Coverdale/Page, Sammy Hagar, Stevie Nicks), Rod Morgenstein (Dixie Dregs, Winger, Jazz Is Dead), and Chris Slade (Tom Jones, Manfred Mann's Earth Band, The Firm, David Gilmour, AC/DC, Asia, Uriah Heep, Gary Numan).

No matter what the musical climate of the day is, there always seems to be a role for the journeyman drummer. In the '80s, many of our greatest players were able to smoothly move between rock, pop, R&B, and even jazz gigs. Omar Hakim, for example, has logged time with Mariah Carey, Weather Report, Madonna, David Bowie, Sting, Miles Davis, and Bruce Springsteen. Meanwhile, Gerry Brown (Stanley Clarke, Stevie Wonder, Diana Ross, Lionel Ritchie), Jonathan Moffet (Madonna, Diana Ross, Elton John), Ricky Lawson (Phil Collins, Michael Jackson, Whitney Houston, Quincy Jones, The Yellowjackets, Steely Dan), and Sonny Emory (Earth Wind & Fire, David Sanborn, Bette Midler, Al Jarreau, Paul Abdul), though often thought of as R&B drummers, have successfully navigated whatever rock and pop environments they've found themselves in.

Today, adaptable rock players like Joey Waronker (Beck, R.E.M., Smashing Pumpkins, Spain, Walt Mink, Elliot Smith), Josh Freese (Suicidal Tendencies, Guns N' Roses, A Perfect Circle, Devo, Ween), Gary Novak (Chick Corea, Alanis Morissette, Robben Ford, David Sanborn, Chaka Khan), and Mitch Marine (Tripping Daisy, David Byrne, Smash Mouth, Dwight Yoakam) prove that the era of the home studio has not completely diminished the need for flexible and creative freelancers. Meanwhile, the highly automated pop music world still finds use for flesh-and-blood drummers to bring the music to life. Witness the full plate of modern players like Teddy Campbell (98 Degrees, Brittney Spears, Rod Stewart, Sisqo, Kelly Clarkson, The Backstreet Boys, Christina Aguilera) and Gerald Heyward (Beyonce, Michael Jackson, Janet Jackson, Missy Elliot, Puff Daddy).

Mitch Marine

# THE GRIP

A drummer's stick grip is his connection to the instrument. Unique, personal, and obsessively analyzed, a player's grip is usually described as "matched," where both hands hold the sticks in the same manner, or "traditional," where the left stick (for righty players) is cradled between the second and third fingers, and wielded with a sort of whipping motion. Old-school drummers tend toward traditional grip, which harks back to the day when military drummers had to angle their snare drums off their legs in order to march and play simultaneously. The creation of the drumset made that grip style unnecessary for all practical purposes. Still, the traditional grip has its adherents to this day, from old-timers who simply play that way out of habit, to young cats trying to cop a classic vibe.

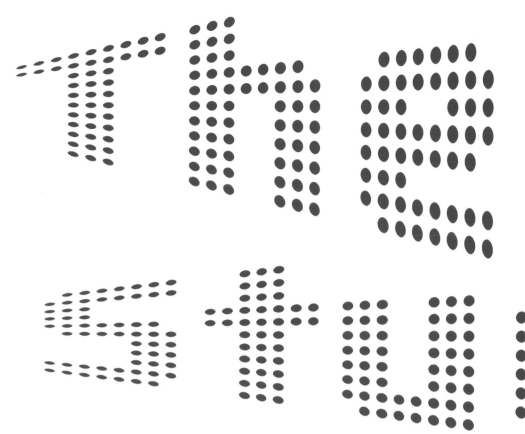

# The Studio

by Ken Micallef

The art of the studio musician truly *is* an art—and not one for the faint of heart or big of head. Beyond the ability to play hot licks—or perhaps in spite of it—the quintessential studio drummer needs great technical control, chart-reading abilities, and the talent to hear what the music needs, almost intuitively.

A studio drummer's grasp of many musical styles and structures must be complete and literally at his fingertips. A sense of dynamics and an ear for tuning are as essential as a solid, unerring time feel. Perhaps most importantly, a studio drummer must be able to suss out the other musicians' (and perhaps the engineer's) needs and musical personalities instantly.

As many musicians have noted, you don't have a great band without an equally great drummer, and in the first-call studio world, that means someone as propulsive and earthy as Earl Palmer or Bernard "Pretty" Purdie, as skillful and innova-

tive as Steve Gadd or Jim Gordon, and as rock solid and raw as Kenny Aronoff, Shawn Pelton, or Jeff Porcaro.

While top contemporary studio drummers like Vinnie Colaiuta, Josh Freese, and Abe Laboriel Jr. are less in demand today than their counterparts during the golden recording era of the '60s, '70s, and '80s, the same rules apply. Sure, today's studio drummer must be comfortable playing along to mechanical "click tracks," and comprehend cutting-edge recording technology. But his most important tools remain his ears, hands, and heart.

The consummate studio drummer understands

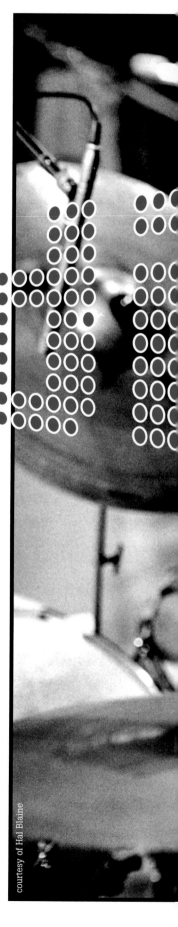

courtesy of Hal Blaine

Hal Blaine "ghost drummed" for many of the great '60s pop-rock bands, and has likely played on more hit songs than any other drummer in history.

# "DRUMS ARE CONVERSATIONAL. IF YOU'RE CONSTANTLY THINKING ABOUT WHAT YOU'RE SAYING, AND NOT LISTENING, THE CONVERSATION SUFFERS."
## —JIM KELTNER

Ebet Roberts

gular drum grooves ever.

Arguably, the first studio drummer was New Orleans' Earl Palmer, the man behind such massive hits as Little Richard's "Lucille," and an eventual studio fixture with Frank Sinatra, The Monkees, Bonnie Raitt, Neil Young, and Elvis Costello, among many others. Palmer's style was visceral and powerful, based on the second-line rhythms of his youth.

A parallel figure on the West Coast was Hal Blaine, a gritty, no-nonsense player whose massively spacious tom fills were often imitated. Blaine is perhaps the most widely recorded studio drummer of all, his earliest dates originating in the 1950s with everyone from Phil Spector and Elvis Presley to The Beach Boys. By his own count, Blaine has recorded over 35,000 tracks.

The modern studio scene began in the 1960s, prompted by Beatlemania and the growth of major

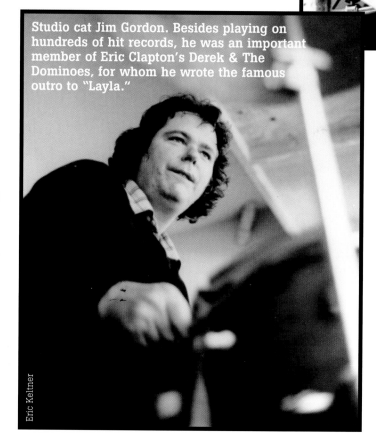

Studio cat Jim Gordon. Besides playing on hundreds of hit records, he was an important member of Eric Clapton's Derek & The Dominoes, for whom he wrote the famous outro to "Layla."

Eric Keltner

the past, the present, and perhaps the future. One drummer who operated in that zone was Jeff Porcaro, who drew from all the drummers he loved. "When I recorded Steely Dan's *Katy Lied*," Jeff recalled in a 1992 *Modern Drummer* magazine article on the drummers of Steely Dan, "all that went through my mind was Jim Keltner and Jim Gordon. All my stuff was from copying them. For instance, on 'Chain Lightning' and 'Black Friday,' all I thought about was Steely Dan's 'Pretzel Logic,' which is Gordon playing a slow shuffle. On 'Doctor Wu,' I was also thinking of John Guerin, who played on Joni Mitchell's *Court And Spark*. 'Your Gold Teeth II' has bars of 3/8, 6/8, and 9/8, which I learned to play by listening to Dannie Richmond play odd meters on a Charles Mingus record. I got frustrated trying to play it, but after walking around the block three times, cursing myself, I came back in and cut it."

Perhaps the greatest West Coast studio drummer of the '70s and '80s, Porcaro respected the studio drummers who had preceded him, while creating one of the most recognizable and sin-

Randy Bachman

record labels on both coasts. Drummers like Jim Keltner and Jim Gordon (who followed in Hal Blaine's footsteps) rose in prominence and workload. Gordon's gifted hands and galloping big beat fueled hits by The Beach Boys, The Byrds, Neil Diamond, and BB King; Keltner recorded with Burt Bacharach, Carly Simon, John Lennon, and Barbra Streisand, to name a few. By the mid 1970s Gordon became afflicted with schizophrenia, but he still recorded with Frank Zappa, Steely Dan, and Derek & The Dominoes, for whom he co-wrote "Layla" with Eric Clapton. Keltner remains a force to this day.

As the music industry grew, including one-hit wonders, soft-rock solo acts, and rock bands that could barely play their way out of a bag, the demand for studio drummers who could "fix" any track grew. Gary Chester, Billy Cobham, Bernard Purdie, Andy Newmark, and Grady Tate dominated New York City, Roger Hawkins ruled laid-back R&B from Muscle Shoals, Al Jackson Jr. hit the mainline with Booker T & The MG's from Memphis, Larry Londin got started in Nashville, Pistol Allen and Benny Benjamin kicked it hard in Motown, and Earl Young, Charles Collins, Norman Farrington, Karl Chambers, and Quinton

Joseph established The Sound Of Philadelphia style with MFSB. In England, Dave Mattacks, Clem Cattini, and Procol Harum's B.J. Wilson showed invention and style on a variety of UK recordings.

As recording sessions became more ambitious, experimental, and intense, studio drummers were required to read almost any drum part—often on the first take. Steve Gadd is legendary for his second-take nail-down of Steely Dan's 1977 classic "Aja," but it was only another day on the job for the most prolific and imitated drummer of the '70s/'80s. Coupling a near-military precision with deep soul and finesse, Gadd was the first-call for pop, jazz, jingles, and everything else.

Other drummers toiling away in New York's plentiful '70s pop-session oven included soul master Steve Jordan, Allan Schwartzberg, Ed Greene, Rick Marotta, Chris Parker, and eventually Yogi Horton, Omar Hakim, and Shawn Pelton. Jazz sessions offered another level of work, and Jeff "Tain" Watts, Victor Lewis, Idris Muhammad, Kenny Washington, Billy Hart, Paul Motian, and Jack DeJohnette laid the path for players like Bill Stewart and Antonio Sanchez.

Rick Gould

**Rick Marotta**

"IF A SINGER
HAS A CERTAIN
STYLE OF
PHRASING,
I WANT TO GET
INTO THAT
STYLE SO I CAN
COMPLEMENT IT
AND PUT THE
DRUMS RIGHT IN
THE POCKET."
—ROGER HAWKINS

Deborah Feingold

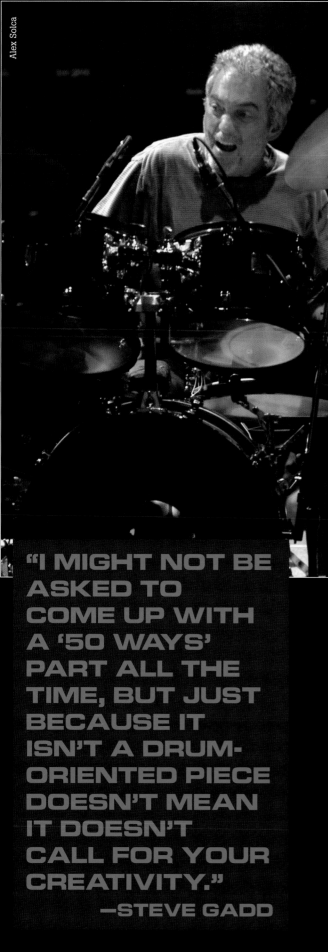

By the early '90s, fueled by a mass exodus of studios to the West Coast and the invasion of the drum machine, drummers skilled in soundtrack work and a smoothness commensurate with hip LA became popular. Los Angeles' biggest studio drum star in the late '70s was Harvey Mason, followed by skilled players like Steve Ferrone, JR Robinson, Denny Fongheiser, and Paul Leim (who eventually became a Nashville fixture).

Today, there is no centralized studio scene per se. At least not in the capacity that existed in the '70s and '80s, when work was so overwhelming that the musicians established a phone bank, The Registry, simply to field all their business calls. Now a small number of elite players handle most of the sessions that aren't coordinated by producers who hire out work to programmers and sample jockeys. The golden age of the studio musician may have passed, but its essence lives on in every drummer who plays purely for the music.

Nashville studio star Eddie Bayers

**"I MIGHT NOT BE ASKED TO COME UP WITH A '50 WAYS' PART ALL THE TIME, BUT JUST BECAUSE IT ISN'T A DRUM-ORIENTED PIECE DOESN'T MEAN IT DOESN'T CALL FOR YOUR CREATIVITY."**
**—STEVE GADD**

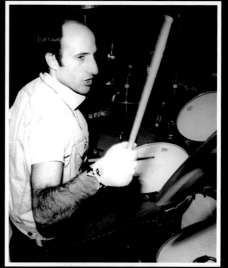

Kenny Aronoff parlayed his gig with John Cougar Mellencamp into one of the fullest schedules of the '80s and '90s studio scene. Known as one of rock's hardest-hitting players, Aronoff in fact spent much of his early training playing legit classical percussion.

# First-call.
# First-take.

Okay, maybe they don't *always* nail the cut on the first pass. But the ability of first-call studio drummers to immediately understand, internalize, and contribute to a song's power and effectiveness, in the pressure-cooker environment of a $300-an-hour recording studio, is truly a wonder of nature. Players like (clockwise, from right) Vinnie Colaiuta, Paul Leim, Matt Chamberlain, and Steve Jordan have earned their remarkable reputations and stayed busy in an incredibly fickle music business by giving producers and artists exactly what they want—fast. In the process, they've exhibited a level of musicality and precision rivaling that of the world's greatest jazz drummers and most sensitive classical percussionists.

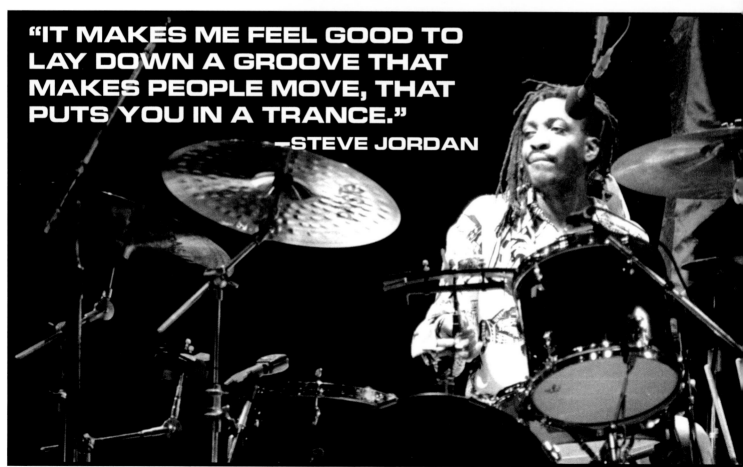

"IT MAKES ME FEEL GOOD TO LAY DOWN A GROOVE THAT MAKES PEOPLE MOVE, THAT PUTS YOU IN A TRANCE."
—STEVE JORDAN

Ebet Roberts

Alex Solca

Alex Solca

In addition to revolutionizing rock
music with his unique beat placement and
distinctive snare sound, Bill Bruford was
an early proponent of electronic drums.

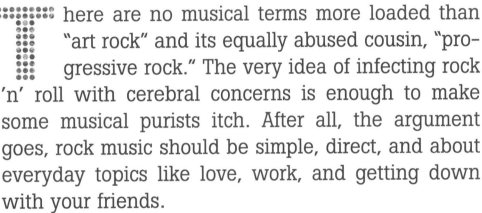

# ROCK

by Adam Budofsky

Don Crispine/Starshotz

There are no musical terms more loaded than "art rock" and its equally abused cousin, "progressive rock." The very idea of infecting rock 'n' roll with cerebral concerns is enough to make some musical purists itch. After all, the argument goes, rock music should be simple, direct, and about everyday topics like love, work, and getting down with your friends.

But the rise of the '60s counterculture made the growing sophistication of rock music unstoppable. Musicians' heads were being blown every day and in every way during the turbulent decade, and the effect of this mind-expansion almost immediately found its way into popular music.

The possibilities facing drummers were now infinite. Players who were increasingly unsatisfied copping Chuck Berry and Jerry Lee Lewis beats were now basking in the freedoms the hippie generation lavished upon them. Audiences didn't just want to dance anymore, they wanted to sit back and listen. All of a sudden, rock drummers had an excuse to *play*.

And that's exactly what they did.

# Unfurling The Freak Flag

**Soft Machine's Robert Wyatt**

Paul Slattery

gious, and philosophical trips, in the process making the charts safe for sitars, political protest, and songs about magic rabbits.

Despite all these musical walls being knocked down, rhythmic experimentation remained relatively tame. Ringo had proven himself an expert accompanist, a songwriter's best friend. But his notable contributions were in the areas of taste, support, and feel, not rhythmic complexity. Likewise, early art rock groups like The Moody Blues (Graeme Edge), Pink Floyd (Nick Mason), and Procol Harum (BJ Wilson) were more about constructing odd pop arrangements and inventing new musical colors than they were about odd time signatures or blazing technical drama. Even the pioneering work of the most avant-garde of America's pop groups, The Velvet Underground (Maureen Tucker) and Frank Zappa's Mothers Of Invention (Jimmy Carl Black), didn't prepare audiences for the drumistic wizardry waiting just around the corner.

**Nick Mason of Pink Floyd**

The seeds of art rock were sewn in the mid-'60s by the two major pillars of modern pop music: Bob Dylan and The Beatles. Dylan had been a hero to the thinking rocker since his earliest albums at the beginning of the decade. But with records like *Bringing It All Back Home*, his lyrics became more playful, surreal, and moody, dramatically expanding the territory songwriters would allow themselves to explore.

Meanwhile, across the ocean, The Beatles' musical ambitions were growing with each new album, as the chamber pop and raga rock of *Rubber Soul* and *Revolver* morphed into the nutty grooviness of *Sgt. Pepper's Lonely Hearts Club Band* and *Magical Mystery Tour*. Psychedelia became the word of the day, and London was the epicenter of all things Day-Glo and freaky.

Back in the States, bands like The Byrds, The Grateful Dead, and The Thirteenth Floor Elevators were writing a distinctly American soundtrack to their generation's new chemical, reli-

# Works In Progress

As the Age Of Aquarius waned and people's tastes shifted (like they always do), the bands who survived Swinging London and San Francisco's Haight-Ashbury scene had a choice to make: Journey further into the murky waters of "progressive" music, or regroup, return to earth, and hone an easier-on-the-ear direction.

Largely, British bands took the former approach, while American bands took the latter. Perhaps it was the Brits' greater sense of ancient history—King Arthur & the Round Table and such—or its booming post-war art school scene. Or maybe it was just that famous British sense of whimsy. Either way, taking pop music into uncharted territory just seemed to make more sense east of the Atlantic.

Robert Wyatt could fairly be described as the Godfather of progressive drumming. As the drummer with influential Canterbury band The Wilde Flowers, and subsequently the kit man and lead singer with Soft Machine (who opened for Jimi Hendrix in 1968), Wyatt broke down doors with his wild, jazz-influenced style. The son of intellectuals with an open-door policy to guests, he absorbed elements of the avant-garde at an early age, and showed an advanced style right from the beginning. Ironically, Wyatt only appreciated pop music later in his career, and following a fall that left him paralyzed below the waist, he began creating much more direct works that featured his uniquely fragile voice. Though he's considered a cult figure in America, Robert Wyatt continues to be a beloved musical icon in Europe, with several bona fide hits as a leader.

By the early '70s, the number of British (and European) bands sporting banks of keyboards, a traveling light show, and multi-part song cycles was staggering. Among the brave drummers who tackled the newly extended track lengths were some fabulously gifted players: Christian Vander (Magma), Pip Pyle (Gong, Hatfield & The North, National Health), Pierre Moerlen (Gong, Mike Oldfield), Jon Hiseman (Colosseum), John Weathers (Gentle Giant), Chris Cutler (Henry Cow/Slapp Happy), Stomu Yamashta (Go!), Michael Giles (King Crimson), and Ron Howden (Nektar) all participated in important albums, each with his own unique sound and style.

The most influential drummers of the golden age of progressive rock were Phil Collins of

Genesis, Clive Bunker and Barriemore Barlow of Jethro Tull, Bill Bruford of Yes and King Crimson, and Carl Palmer of ELP and Asia. Collins, a child actor and Mod enthusiast, joined Genesis for their third album, *Nursery Cryme*, and helped catapult that band to international fame. Besides a great feel, Collins' style featured quick footwork, uniquely effective accents, and burning fills that suggested an affinity for the fusion style of Mahavishnu's Billy Cobham. He also had an effective singing voice, which would

Though he would later make his name as a superstar singer-songwriter, Phil Collins came to prominence as a highly creative drummer with Genesis.

Ross Halfin/Idols

serve him quite well in the '80s, when his successful solo career blossomed and Genesis enjoyed their biggest hits. Collins' sound, with its tell-tale single-headed tom attack, is famously preserved on mid-period Genesis albums like *A Trick Of The Tail* (his lead-singer maiden voyage, following the departure of Peter Gabriel) and on the first single from his solo debut, "In The Air Tonight," which features one of the most famous air-drumming moments of modern recording.

# "I FIND THE FEELING THAT A MUSICIAN IS HOLDING BACK ATTRACTIVE. THE FEELING THAT SOMETHING IS THERE AND COULD COME OUT IN LITTLE BITS AT ANY MOMENT IS ATTRACTIVE TO ME."
## —BILL BRUFORD

Like many British art rock bands, Jethro Tull began as a blues- and jazz-influenced combo. They quickly expanded their style to include elements of British folk, classical, and hard rock, and captured the imagination of FM radio listeners with 1971's *Aqualung*, a concept album that featured many staples of the group's live repertoire. *Aqualung* was in fact the last Tull studio album to feature the work of their original drummer, Clive Bunker, an intense groover who at times could evoke the humanistic crunch of Led Zeppelin's John Bonham. In his floppy farmer's hat, Bunker was a bundle of energy, and can be heard to great effect on his drum feature from *Living In The Past*, "Dharma For One."

Carl Palmer of ELP:
Bigger is often better.

Brian Killigrew

Michael S. Jachles

**Alan White of Yes**

Bunker was succeeded by Barriemore Barlow, a quite different yet equally shocking player. With a massive kit and laser-precision chops, Barlow embraced Tull's increasingly complex arrangements and added an unpredictability and strangeness to the band's rhythms—which were *already* out of this world. Barlow, a wizard at odd times and dramatic flourishes, can best be heard on Tull's most ambitious works, the album-length pieces *Thick As A Brick* and *A Passion Play*.

Yes burst on the scene with a jones for The Beatles, Leonard Bernstein, and the infinite variables of musical color. After a couple of albums spent finding their feet, the group hit pay dirt with *The Yes Album*, which included the epic pieces "Starship Trooper," "Yours Is No Disgrace," and "I've Seen All Good People." Powering these ultra-dramatic yarns was Bill Bruford, whose absorption of the odd-time chamber-jazz albums of Dave Brubeck

(with Joe Morello) provided him with a unique slant on beat placement. Bruford could be immediately identified by his ringing snare drum and constantly shifting approach to rhythm, which made him one of the most revered drummers of the era.

Bruford left Yes at the height of their success to join the more avant-garde King Crimson, where he further redefined the art of art-rock drumming. Bruford's replacement in Yes was John Lennon/George Harrison vet Alan White, a tumbling, tricky, and tribal drummer (and accomplished keyboard player) who remains with the band to this day. Bruford, whose seminal progressive recordings include Yes's *Close To The Edge* and Crimson's *Red* and *Discipline*, would eventually go on to lead his own jazz band, Earthworks. When he exited Crimson in the '90s, he left the band in the capable hands and feet of Pat Mastelotto, whose well of clever ideas and embrace of electronic technology make him one

of the most fascinating drummers of modern times.

In a genre of bombastic ideals, perhaps the *most* bombastic band was Emerson, Lake & Palmer. A "supergroup" featuring players from British musical institutions The Nice, King Crimson, and Atomic Rooster (respectively), ELP featured the rhythmic histrionics of Carl Palmer. Palmer clearly listened to his share of Buddy Rich performances, eliciting a passion and chops-heavy approach that more than adequately filled the huge arenas the massively popular ELP played. With his famous stainless-steel drumkit, obligatory gong, and complete willingness to solo like the cops were after him, Palmer took ELP mini-suites like "Tarkus," "Karn Evil 9," and "Pictures At An Exhibition" to stratospheric heights, and slayed legions of up-and-coming drummers with his larger-than-life musical personality. Palmer would see even further success in the '80s with another supergroup, Asia.

Jaki Liebezeit of Can.
German precision coupled
with an authentic—and
oft-sampled—groove.

*Courtesy of Spoon Records*

Phil Ehart of Kansas

# Can't Stop Progress

Finally dragged down by its own heaviosity, the original pro-gressive rock sound fell out of favor around 1976/77 with the arrival of punk and new wave. (You could probably hear *that* thump on Saturn.) But the ideals of experimentation and musical ambition did not die with it.

Reflecting the influences of free-jazz and twentieth-century classical composers like Steve Reich, John Cage, and Karlheinz Stockhausen, a German out-rock genre later dubbed (unfortunate-ly) Krautrock supplied adventurous listeners with some of the most uncompromising and creative sounds of the '70s. Between the man-machine rhythms of Kraftwerk's Wolfgang Flur, the *motorik* beats of Neu!'s Klaus Dinger, and the wondrous dada explosion that was Faust (featuring Werner "Zappi" Diermaier), Krautrock offered an adventurous vision that managed to avoid the lyrical trappings and chops-for-chops'-sake pitfalls of early art rock. Perhaps the most appealing drumming of the style was provided by Can's Jaki Liebezeit, an ex–free jazz player who had the time of a stop-watch, the groove of a James Brown drummer,

and the trance-inducing abilities of a shaman. Liebezeit and Can's long-lasting impact on modern music was proven in the late '90s, when electronic artists could often be heard dropping their name—and sampling their beats.

In America, Frank Zappa held a unique and unparalleled posi-tion in the hearts and minds of forward-thinking musicians, with a work ethic and inquisitive nature that was almost unimagin-able. Obviously, Zappa's drummers had to pull their weight, and between the pliable slam of Aynsley Dunbar, the theatricality of Terry Bozzio, the not-of-this-earth ideas of Vinnie Colaiuta, and the technical leaps of Chad Wackerman, you could almost guar-antee a healthy number of drum geeks at any Zappa show, down by the stage, drooling.

Neil Peart of Rush

Jerry Marotta with
Peter Garbiel

Mike Portnoy of
Dream Theater

Mike Haid

Anton Fier (The Feelies, Lounge Lizards, Golden Palominos) were all important parts of the New York avant-garde rock community, and David Licht (Shockabilly, Bongwater) and Scott Krauss (Pere Ubu) confirmed that alternative rock could handle some crazy rhythms as well.

Surprisingly, the biggest name in prog-rock drumming came from up in Canada. Rush, featuring Neil Peart, based their sound on the blueprints laid out by Genesis and Yes, but added a more futuristic metallic sheen and a clear-as-day adherence to odd-time mania. Peart, a formidable soloist, quickly became the most obsessed-over drummer of his generation, eliciting more fan mail and critical discussion than any other drummer of the day. Neil and Rush still tour and put out popular albums, continually confounding the naysayers who thought prog died three decades ago.

Despite Rush's popularity, as the '70s moved into the '80s, the classic progressive style had all but disappeared, though not without strong efforts by Kansas (with Phil Ehart), Marillion (featuring Ian Mosely), Fates Warning (Mark Zonder), Queensrÿche (Scott Rockenfield), and later, the drummer many consider the logical extension of Neil Peart, Mike Portnoy of Dream Theater.

Though discussion of the '80s music scene usually focuses on new wave and disco, the spirit of adventure lived on in strange corners of rock music. Jerry Marotta and Manu Katché helped Peter Gabriel establish a unique sound beyond Genesis, David Van Tieghem (Laurie Anderson, Brian Eno), Fred Maher (Material), and

In the mid-'80s, industrial rock, in the hands of Ministry (Bill Rieflin), Nine Inch Nails (Chris Vrenna), Skinny Puppy (cEvin Key), and Pigface (Martin Atkins), though all about metal riffs and jack-hammer beats, also pointed to new directions in beatsmanship. Late in the decade, the so-called math-rock scene featured bands like Shellac (Todd Trainer), Slint (Britt Walford), and Rapeman (Rey Washam), whose complexity was only outshone by their brutality.

The '90s brought a more melodious wave of forward-lookers, in Chicago avant-rock purveyors The Sea And Cake and Tortoise (renaissance man John McEntire), Wilco (the extra-creative Glenn Kotche), and the French band Air, which featured electronic whiz and soundtrack producer Brian Reitzell. All these bands provided much momentum for the shocking sounds to come in the new millennium, such as Danny Carey's Tool and Jon Theodore's Mars Volta. The gargantuan performances of drummers like these prove that, whatever box you want to place them in, rock musicians will always be hungry for the sound of progress.

# "I COULDN'T STOP PLAYING HARD PHYSICALLY, BECAUSE I LOVE PHYSICAL EXERTION IN SO MANY OTHER AREAS OF MY LIFE. AND THAT ACTUALLY CAME FROM DRUMMING."
## —NEIL PEART

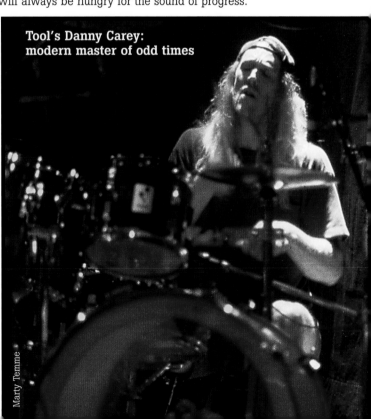

Tool's Danny Carey:
modern master of odd times

Marty Temme

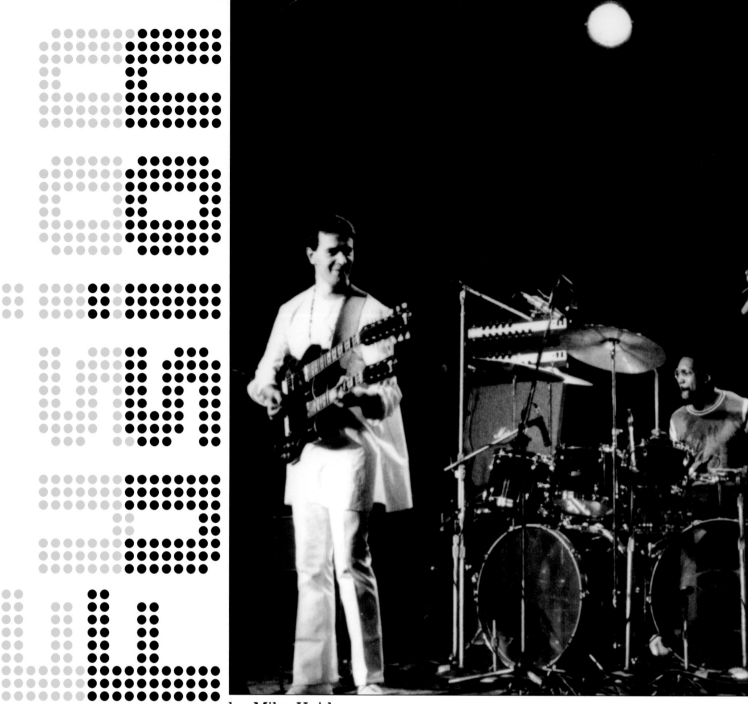

by Mike Haid

It was 1970-something. I turned the TV to my regular late-night weekend music program, *In Concert*, to catch up on the latest rock bands, always searching for another inspirational drummer. What appeared on the screen was life-altering. A clean-cut guitar player, dressed like a guru in all white linen cloth, with unusually short hair and a double-neck guitar, was playing faster—*much* faster—and with just as much passion as Hendrix, Page, or Jeff Beck.

But it was the drummer who pulled me out of my chair, onto my knees,

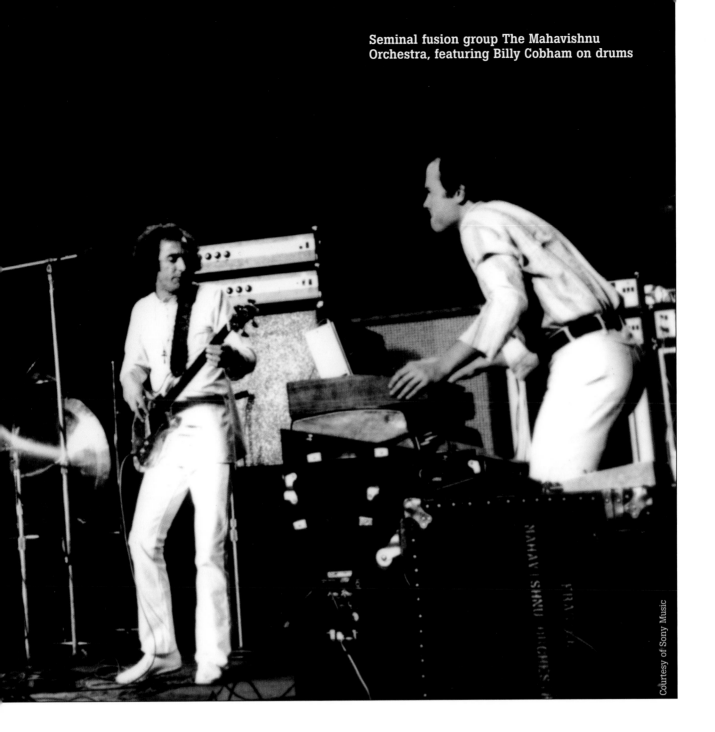

Courtesy of Sony Music

in front of the TV screen. A dude who looked like a bodybuilder was attacking an enormous double bass drumkit with the power and speed of Muhammed Ali during a title bout. His ferocity, his agility, and the technical facility of his hands and feet were superhuman. This addictive, amazingly intense, and complex style of rock was from another planet. I had to find this Mahavishnu Orchestra record the next day.

Witnessing Billy Cobham's attitude and abilities, I had found my calling as a drummer. It was jazz-rock fusion.

After gaining international exposure with '80s arena-rock hit-makers Journey, Steve Smith became a fusion drumming icon with his group Vital Information. Smith's relaxed control while negotiating complex parts is legendary, while his recent explorations of Indian rhythms is pushing drumset music into exciting new territories.

It was 1980-something. I was attending a music trade show and stepped into a room where a young drummer that I had heard good things about was performing.

When Vinnie Colaiuta began to play, I was speechless. He had all the intensity and blistering chops of the greatest jazz, rock, and Latin drummers that I had ever heard, fused into a style that was incomprehensible.

In my mind, I flashed back to that first image of Billy Cobham on TV. That same alien feeling came over me, as Colaiuta's vicious, commanding, unrelenting exploratory attitude grabbed me by the throat. It has never let go.

It was 1990-something. A hot Cuban drummer had been drawing attention in the fusion community. I picked up a CD he was on and began listening. The drummer was certainly excellent, but I couldn't understand quite what all the fuss was about.

As I checked the liner notes to see which percussionists were playing along with him, the only name I saw listed in the credits was Horacio "El Negro" Hernandez. I was in denial and disbelief—until I saw him perform. Not only does "El Negro" pos-

sess amazing jazz/rock/Latin drumset chops, he layers and weaves sophisticated percussion parts into his grooves and solos that must be seen to be believed. Horacio is credited for introducing the popular left-foot cowbell/clave technique, a milestone in fusion history.

In the new millennium, a developing fourth generation of fusion drumming from like-minded innovators continues to bring us to our knees, challenging us to explore uncharted rhythmic worlds. This is the undying enchantment of fusion drumming, which continues to increase readership of drum magazines and fill concert halls for clinics and drum festivals. Fusion is addictive, and it *rocks*.

The rhythmic fire was set ablaze when jazz icon Miles Davis recorded his legendary *Bitches Brew* sessions in 1969, fusing rock, funk, and jazz into an electrifying new sound labeled jazz-rock fusion. The collaborative efforts of young jazz pioneers playing electronic instruments on these sessions would spawn three influential fusion super-groups in the '70s: Joe Zawinul and Wayne Shorter's Weather Report, Chick Corea's Return To Forever, and John McLaughlin's Mahavishnu Orchestra.

Although Miles is historically credited for the birth of fusion, it was Miles' former drummer, Tony Williams, who in 1969 paved the way for the powerful jazz-rock drumming style with his Lifetime trio, which included keyboardist Larry Young and brilliant English guitarist John McLaughlin (who declined joining Miles Davis to work with Lifetime). On their first recording, *Emergency!*, Williams clearly states his intentions of smashing the lock on traditional jazz drumming. Tony drove his advanced, exploratory rhythmic concepts—and volume levels—to

Australian drummer Virgil Donati is an intense chops monster who routinely leaves drummers scratching their heads at his otherworldly kit work.

extreme heavy-rock proportions within genre-crossing compositions, in counterpoint to British rock drummers like Ginger Baker and John Bonham, who were weaving jazz influences into their creative rock drumming approach.

Williams, only twenty-four years old in 1969, had been working for the previous seven years with Miles in the highly cele-

Alex Solca

**Dave Weckl's fluid approach to electric jazz, open sound, and skill at soloing over vamps made him the most imitated drummer of his generation.**

brated jazz quintet that also featured Wayne Shorter, Herbie Hancock, and Ron Carter. Tony was heavily influenced by rock artists from The Beatles to Jimi Hendrix, and he was willing to throw his sophisticated jazz chops into the popular rock arena to try to connect with his generation of rock music listeners.

Miles had the clout to bring fusion to the masses, but Williams brought the intensity and authentic rock attitude into jazz, opening the flood gates of improvisational jazz/rock drumming concepts that continue to inspire and influence drummers of all genres. Although the Lifetime trio was short-lived due to poor management, jazz-rock fusion continued to gain popularity among the young rock audience in the '70s.

As Miles gradually fell off the fusion charts, the groups that formed out of the *Bitches Brew* sessions gained momentum. The next drummer to step into the limelight was Panama-born Billy Cobham, teamed with former Lifetime guitarist John McLaughlin in his new Mahavishnu Orchestra.

Cobham's explosive double bass drumming lit up the stage—as did his huge drumkit, unbridled speed and precision, and complex, rudimental, polyrhythmic style. Watching Cobham and McLaughlin was like watching two superheroes battle, pushing each other's technical and physical abilities to the absolute limit.

Cobham would set out on his own to record the pivotal *Spectrum* LP, a much funkier, more rock-oriented collection than

## SIMON PHILLIPS' "SPACE BOOGIE"

In the late '70s and early '80s, young British session drummer Simon Phillips became highly in-demand, turning heads with his adventurous, musical approach by incorporating innovative double bass grooves, challenging fills, and complex rhythmic patterns. One of Simon's most memorable efforts, "Space Boogie," appeared on guitar legend Jeff Beck's classic 1980 release, *There And Back*. On the cut, Simon creates a mind-blowing, uptempo double bass shuffle groove in 7/4, featuring a traditional swing cymbal pattern and backbeat accents on 2, 4, and 6, with (unaccented) ghost notes on the snare. The tune's arrangement actually shifts between sections of 7/4 and 4/4.

In a 1998 interview in *Fuse* magazine, Simon, who co-wrote half of the eight songs on *There And Back,* recalled the creation of this historic track: "We were at Jeff Beck's house, and it was a very casual thing. I brought a small Ludwig single-bass drumkit, and Jeff had a small single-bass Premier kit there as well. I wanted to expand my kit a little, so I grabbed a bass drum and a tom from his kit and added them to mine. We started messing around, playing a fast boogie shuffle similar to Billy Cobham's 'Quadrant 4.' I started turning it around by playing seven across the four, which was the kind of thing that I did all the time. I kept playing in seven while the others played through the changes, but Jeff sort of went with me and then stopped and said, "Wow, that's great! Play it again." So we played it again, and I put it into my mental notebook. [Keyboardist] Tony Hymas and I worked out the arrangement later, and when we played it for Jeff, he loved it."

Today "Space Boogie" is considered one of the most influential double bass fusion grooves in drumming history.

courtesy of Tama/Hoshino

Ebet Roberts

**"A LOT OF PEOPLE SAID IT WAS A GOD-GIVEN TALENT, BUT I WAS ALWAYS PRACTICING. I WOULD GET UP IN THE SUMMERTIME AND HOP RIGHT ON THE KIT AND NOT STOP UNTIL SUNDOWN."**
**—DENNIS CHAMBERS**

any Mahavishnu recording. This captured the ears of rock fans, due in large part to the gritty blues-rock guitar work of Tommy Bolin. This recording also nudged guitar legend Jeff Beck into exploring this music further. Beck created several noteworthy fusion recordings featuring Cobham's Mahavishnu replacement drummer, Narada Michael Walden, as well as the virtually unknown Richard Bailey, Ed Greene, Tony Smith, and young British studio phenom Simon Phillips. Phillips and Walden would continue to explore jazz-rock drumming on their own noteworthy recordings.

Chick Corea's Latin-flavored fusion group Return To Forever featured Brazilian drummer/percussionist Airto Moreira, taking a listener-friendly Latin-jazz direction. The next phase of RTF

would prove highly successful with its neatly structured, challenging classical/jazz/rock/funk/Latin arrangements, which introduced the clean, tight, funky drumming of Lenny White. The rhythm section of White, bassist extraordinaire Stanley Clarke, and guitar whiz Al Di Meola would electrify audiences and bring a new level of technical proficiency to fusion.

Corea had originally hired Rochester, New York drummer Steve Gadd to join RTF, but at the time Gadd was not interested in touring, and was replaced by White. Corea later released masterful solo recordings with Gadd that would seal the drummer's legacy as an innovator, with his unsurpassed versatility, unique drum sound, and uncanny compositional drumming concepts.

In the '80s, Corea would assemble another successful fusion project. The Chick Corea Elektric Band incorporated a more modern, sophisticated electronic jazz sound with the innovative acoustic/electric drum setup of Dave Weckl, whose advanced techniques descended from the Gadd school. Today Weckl continues to explore new directions in fusion with his own group.

The Zawinul/Shorter Weather Report was more eclectic than the other early fusion groups, involving more percussive, ethnic rhythms. The group originally featured Airto Moreira (later replaced by Dom Um Romao) and the flamboyant drummer Alphonse Mouzon, who, like Cobham, played a large double bass kit with speed, agility, and aggression. Mouzon also had success with his powerful, funky double bass technique in guitarist Larry Coryell's Eleventh House.

Mouzon would eventually be replaced in Weather Report by sophisticated Philadelphia drummer Eric Gravatt. In fact, Weather Report went through many excellent drummers, including Sly Stone's Gregg Errico, Herschell Dwellingham, Ishmael Wilburn, Skip Hadden, Darryl Brown, Leon "Ndugu"

# LA's Historic Fusion Hang

Greg Mathieson    Abraham Laboriel
Michael Landau    Vinnie Colaiuta

For over thirty years, the Baked Potato, a tiny, unassuming nightclub in North Hollywood, California, has been host to the biggest names in fusion drumming. Owner Don Randi, an accomplished keyboard player, has made it a point to showcase the cream of the crop in Los Angeles jazz/rock/Latin/funk fusion music. In the '80s, the late, great drummers Jeff Porcaro and Carlos Vega appeared regularly. Today, on any given night you might find Alex Acuña, Vinnie Colaiuta, Virgil Donati, Dave Weckl, Simon Phillips, or Gregg Bissonette jamming with top local session players.

This landmark for fusion aficionados has also produced some amazing live recordings, most notably *Live At The Baked Potato 2000*, which features some ferocious fusion drumming from the legendary Vinnie Colaiuta.

# "I JUST DON'T FEEL GOOD UNLESS I PLAY FOR AN HOUR A DAY. IF I DON'T PLAY FOR THREE DAYS, I START TO GET ANTSY AND FEEL OUT OF KILTER."

## —TERRY BOZZIO

Chancler, Chester Thompson, Alex Acuña, Peter Erskine, and Omar Hakim.

Jack DeJohnette was another one of the era's hot drummers. Jack's impressionistic playing with saxophonist Charles Lloyd hinted at rock flavorings, but was firmly grounded in jazz, which earned him a pivotal role in Miles Davis's *Bitches Brew* sessions along with Cobham and Lenny White. Other influential fusion drummers include Harvey Mason and Mike Clark, both of whom created deep-pocket funk grooves for keyboardist Herbie Hancock's classic Headhunter recordings, developing a strong backbeat for a new fusion direction. This approach resulted in fusion finding its way onto FM radio, where it enjoyed much success in the '70s.

This new level of popularity wasn't all good for the music, though. Due to record-label demands for more radio-friendly sounds, the spirited composition and musical adventure had been drained from most fusion music by the mid-'80s, with only a few die-hard pioneers remaining. A funkier, more backbeat-driven strain of fusion would eventually grow in popularity, with artists like David Sanborn, Lee Ritenour, George Benson, and Dave Grusin, and groups like Spyro Gyra, Wishful Thinking, and Yellowjackets developing a more homogeneous style known as smooth jazz, or contemporary jazz, which continues to find mass appeal in the over-thirty radio market.

Despite the watering down of fusion in some circles, the original drumming style is alive and well, and it remains one of the most influential and inspiring styles of drumming on the planet. Present-day players who've dedicated their careers to the advancement of fusion drumming include Paul Wertico, Terry Bozzio, Bill Bruford, Billy Cobham, Vinnie Colaiuta, Dennis Chambers,

Kirk Covington, Gary Husband, Paco Sery, Steve Smith, Trilok Gurtu, Chad Wackerman, Simon Phillips, and Dave Weckl.

And a new breed of international fusion drummers continues to incorporate many unique and challenging techniques. This list of rhythmic magicians includes Virgil Donati, Rodney Holmes, Marco Minnemann, Thomas Lang, Mike Mangini, Horacio "El Negro" Hernandez, Jimmy Branly, Akira Jimbo, Jojo Mayer, Keith Carlock, Gene Lake, Sean Rickman, Antonio Sanchez, Jeff Ballard, and Joel Taylor. These drummers and others further an unlimited range of global musical influences, pushing the technical demands of tomorrow's fusion drummer into far-reaching, ever-expanding, and mentally challenging directions.

**Weather Report's Omar Hakim. His solo on Sting's "I Burn For You" from the live album Bring On The Night was an MTV highlight in 1986.**

Joost Leijen

# Latin

by Martin Patmos

Latin drumset grooves have become an important part of drumming vocabulary. While for better or worse any rhythm coming from the Caribbean or South America is often lumped under the term "Latin," Afro-Cuban and Brazilian rhythms are the most well known. Challenging and inspiring, these grooves evolved from the mix of African and Spanish or African and Portuguese cultures.

Tom Copi

Sheila E: drummer, star

Originally played on congas, cowbells, and other percussion instruments, these grooves have gradually been adapted to the drumset. Whether its a mambo, cha cha cha, rhumba, Afro-Cuban 6/8 feel, bossa nova, samba, or something else, drumset interpretations have evolved to carry on the feel of these rhythms. And while sometimes these drumset grooves are played along with other percussionists, when solo, the drummer has the opportunity to orchestrate the traditional percussion parts around the kit, requiring dexterity and interdependence.

Since much of Latin pop sticks to traditional instrumentation or uses programmed sounds, perhaps the largest use of these rhythms for drumset can be found in Latin-jazz, where it is a key component of the rhythm section. Early on, Afro-Cuban jazz practically always used traditional percussion. But in the time it has developed since the 1950s, there's been a shift to make much more use of the drumset. Added to that, the early-'60s Brazilian music craze introduced samba and bossa nova to the drummer's Latin repertoire. In playing these diverse styles, many of today's drummers augment their drumsets, including cowbells, woodblocks, timbales, and other mounted percussion instruments.

The fascination with applying Latin rhythms to the drumset reached a high point in the late '80s, due to the highly evolved concepts of fusion players like Dave Weckl, who inspired many young, chops-hungry imitators.

Mimmo Urz

Horacio "El Negro" Hernandez, the spirit of Tito Puente never far behind, sent thousands of drummers back to the woodshed with his method of playing the foundational Latin rhythm, clave, with his left foot on a pedal-operated cowbell.

There are many capable drummers playing and teaching these styles today, with several excellent and inspiring players leading the way. Perhaps most notable is Horacio "El Negro" Hernandez, who around 1990 seemingly burst forth from Cuba deftly playing clave with his left foot. In doing so, he challenged many with his coordination, while permanently impacting Latin drumset method.

Another important player is Steve Berrios, who has perfected the transition between Afro-Cuban and Jazz rhythms with a deep, earthy style. Ignacio Berroa, Bobby Sanabria, and Vince Cherico are other important players. From Brazil are Airto Moreira, famous for his sense of color, while Dom Um Romao and Duduka Da Fonseca have explored Brazilian drumset possibilities in other ways. Alex Acuña, originally from Peru, brought his wealth of knowledge to fusion, just as Antonio Sanchez is bringing his knowledge to many exciting projects today.

As the youngest member of the Latin percussion section, the drumset has quickly proven itself as an adaptable, energetic instrument offering many possibilities. The works of such master percussionists as timbalero Tito Puente and congueros Carlos "Potato" Valdez, Francisco Aguabella, Poncho Sanchez, Ray Barretto, and Giovanni Hidalgo offer plenty of inspiration. Yet the Afro-Latin grooves of the drumset—with their blend of energy, coordination, tradition, and depth—offer a nearly unparalleled fascination to drummers the world over.

Seth Cashman

Walfredo de los Reyes is often acknowledged as the originator of mixing traditional Latin percussion with drumset.

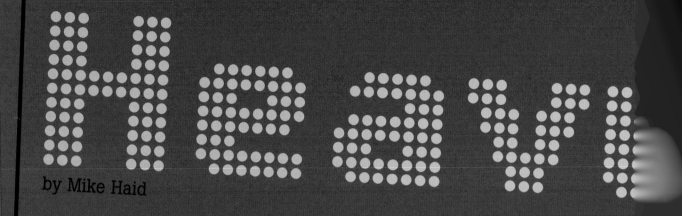

# Heavy

by Mike Haid

**Heavy metal drumming is a test of** stamina, athleticism, speed, **and** agility. **It is clearly the most physical style of drumming, typically based on** molten **feels laced with** energetic **combination** fills **and** abundant cymbal crashes.

# Metal

Ian Paice of Deep Purple. Metal drumming starts here.

# "I JUST CAN'T SIT AND BE QUIET ON A SET OF DRUMS. IF I SIT AT THE DRUMS, I HAVE TO BE LOUD."
## —CHARLIE BENANTE

**Alex Van Halen.** The shuffling double bass drum intro to Van Halen's "Hot For Teacher" confounded many a nascent headbanger.

In the early '70s, rock music was getting louder and more visual, as new directions in style and emotion were being explored. Metal was born from British rock bands forging a darker, guitar-oriented style with a driving groove. Typical metal songs usually featured powerful double bass drumming or a slow, hammering dirge-like groove with a thick, wall-of-guitar backdrop and screaming upper-register vocals.

Give most of the credit to British rock legends Black Sabbath and Deep Purple for inspiring the classic heavy metal sound that we know today. Sabbath offered dark, mysterious melodies with macabre lyrics, as vocalist Ozzy Osbourne touched a demonic nerve. Drummer Bill Ward played with a loose and at times adventurous technique that seemed jazz-inspired. At the same time, seasoned British rock group Deep Purple brought a burning, heavy sound that featured up-tempo, driving rhythms with grinding Hammond organ and the virtuoso guitar work of Ritchie Blackmore, offering classically based melody lines at blinding speeds. This gave drummer Ian Paice the perfect canvas to create his technically advanced, jazz-influenced, high-velocity grooves and fills.

Combining the technical creativity and vocal intensity of Deep Purple with the evil edge of Black Sabbath was Judas Priest. The sound that Priest created ushered in the era of true heavy metal, as the band, dressed in black leather and metal studs, gave this new genre an iron-clad image and a thunderous, heart-pounding sound. Priest went through several great drummers, including Alan Moore, young session drummer Simon Phillips, Les Binks, Dave Holland, and Scott Travis. Each drummer brought an element of intensity and individual style that clearly defined the molten groove of heavy metal's most influential group.

Other groups that pioneered the early era of metal include

Saxon, Rainbow, Mötörhead, Scorpions, The Michael Schenker Group, Iron Maiden, and UFO. Outstanding drummers that helped shape the early metal sound were legendary freelancers like Cozy Powell, Tommy Aldridge, Carmine Appice, and Aynsley Dunbar, and Nicko McBrain with Iron Maiden.

The '80s wave of heavy metal was focused on American bands. Los Angeles was a hotbed for metal in the Me Decade, as successful groups like Van Halen (Alex Van Halen) and Mötley Crüe

(Tommy Lee) brought the style into the pop mainstream. MTV continued to emphasize popular music as a visual art form, and the so-called "hair bands" became an overnight success. Groups like Bon Jovi, Def Leppard, Dokken, Ratt, Poison, Stryper, Winger, Cinderella, Quiet Riot, Twisted Sister, Skid Row, Whitesnake, and Zebra were constantly in regular rotation. Heavier acts like Dio, WASP, Mötörhead, Y&T, Scorpions, Judas Priest, and Ozzy were staples on MTV's late-night *Headbanger's Ball* show.

As the '80s wore on and mainstream metal became more commercial, new sub-genres surfaced with more aggressive, angrier attitudes. Regardless of what direction metal drumming takes, though, precision, volume, and speed remain its core traits.

Gene Ambo

Tommy Lee

Paul Natkin/Photofeatures Int.

# Bigger

Throughout the history of rock, as music became louder, drummers were forced to keep up with the volume by playing with continuously heavier, more aggressive techniques. The early drum manufacturers designed their hardware for subtle jazz drumming, which was not holding up to the punishment of this new generation of rock slammers. To withstand the onslaught, the Tama company introduced heavier, "double-braced" stands, which were less likely to tip over and cause all kinds of

Nick Menza of Megadeth

# Heavier Faster Louder!

damage. (A 20"-diameter rock crash cymbal toppling over could cut a power line like a knife through butter!)

As rock music became even more adventurous, drummers began expanding the size of their kits as well. Early rock pioneers like Ginger Baker (Cream) and Carmine Appice (Vanilla Fudge), fusioneers Billy Cobham, Alphonse Mouzon, Chester Thompson, Narada Michael Walden, Simon Phillips, and Terry Bozzio, and progressive rock gods Carl Palmer and Neil Peart created huge setups incorporating an array of percussion. The Ludwig drum company came out with its massive Octa-Plus drumkit, which featured eight single-headed concert toms and a choice of one or two bass drums. Today, new hardware technology continues to increase the size of drumkits in the way of multiple foot pedals, stand-mounted percussion, a variety of snare drums, and tons of cymbal options. Among the most notable massive kits of recent years are Mike Portnoy's "Siamese Monster" and Terry Bozzio's unique melodic one-man percussion orchestra kit.

Ross Halfin/Idols

**Nicko McBrain, poster boy for the monstrous multi-tom kit**

Funk is, as the great James Brown horn
man Maceo Parker proclaims, happy
music. The changes may be the blues, but
the beat is a party goin' on. For drummers
it allows creativity: off-beat, in between
the beat, behind the beat, ahead of the
beat playing. You get the idea: The beat is
a toy, and it's all in the context of a
super-strong pocket. **by Robin Tolleson**

Bernard Purdie. How many
other drummers have a beat
named after them?

# "GIVING THE DRUMMER SOME," A FOUR- OR EIGHT-MEASURE DRUM OR RHYTHM SECTION FEATURE, BECAME AN ACCEPTED, EVEN ANTICIPATED PART OF MANY FUNK TUNES.

A sampler's treasure trove: James Brown's Clyde Stubblefield...

Paul La Raia

Funk invaded the AM airwaves in the late 1960s, as James Brown's message got more political and his music got more rhythmically exciting. "Cold Sweat" made America break out, and long-time JB drummers Melvin Parker, Clyde Stubblefield, and John "Jabo" Starks kept upping the groove bar with syncopated beats that emphasized off-beat punches, barking hi-hats, a super-tight snare, and a thick kick. "Giving the drummer some," a four- or eight-measure drum or rhythm section feature, became an accepted, even anticipated part of many funk tunes. Check out Dwight Burns on Archie Bell & The Drells' "Tighten Up," Stubblefield's "Funky Drummer" groove with James Brown, and GC Coleman's drum break on the Winstons' "Amen Brother." Full of feeling *and* precision, these would become the most sampled breaks in the hip-hop era.

Other funk forerunners include Sly & The Family Stone, who emerged in 1968 thanking us for letting them be themselves, with drummers Greg Errico and Andy Newmark. Tower Of Power's David Garibaldi, whose creative, linear, rudimental funk feel has been much imitated, was closely followed by the deep pockets of David Bartlett and Ronnie Beck in the San Francisco Bay area. Joseph "Zigaboo" Modeliste created several all-time grooves in the '70s with The Meters, proving that 2 & 4 could be implied instead of played without sacrificing the flow. (Check out the cut "Rejuvenation.") George Clinton's Parliament-Funkadelic collective always boasted some of the funkiest drummers, including Jerome "Bigfoot" Brailey, Raymond "Tiki" Fulwood (*One Nation Under A Groove*), Tyrone Lampkin, and a young Dennis Chambers (*Live At The Beverly Theatre*).

In the early '70s, Robbie McIntosh and Steve Ferrone took hi-hat work to another level with Average White Band, and Raymond Pounds gave Stevie Wonder's *Songs In The Key Of Life* its groove. Andre Fisher, Richard "Moon" Calhoun, and then John "J.R." Robinson gave Rufus (featuring Chaka Khan) its big beats, while James "Diamond" Williams forged new funk with Ohio Players.

Jazz musicians began seeing the potential for electric funk improvisations in the '70s, as acts like The Crusaders, Herbie Hancock's Headhunters, and Donald Byrd featured drummers like Stix Hooper, Harvey Mason, and Mike Clark. Jazz-trained keyboardist George Duke and bassist Stanley Clarke banded together in the name of funk, and George and Louis Johnson, two of Quincy Jones' favorite session players, scored big with "Get The Funk Out Ma Face" and "Strawberry Letter #23" as The Brothers Johnson.

Ndugu Chancler did some great funk drumming on George Duke's early albums (*I Love The Blues, She Heard My Cry*), and injected Michael Jackson's "Billie Jean" with some real snap. Drummer Ron Beitle and the band Wild Cherry had a smash with the engaging raw pop sound of "Play That Funky Music," and Earth Wind & Fire had big pop-funk hits with Maurice White, Ralph Johnson, and Fred White laying it down.

... and John "Jabo" Starks

Paul La Raia

The disco era rose out of funk, bringing a specific set of demands on the kit player. Soon, however, the very mention of the "D" word became dreaded by drummers because of the often monotonous, non-playful nature of the grooves. That, and the fact that it foreshadowed the pre-hatched drum machine parts that took work away from live players in the ensuing years.

The 1980s and '90s saw several good funk groups and drummers hanging on in the face of higher bpms, including "Mean" Willie Green with The Neville Brothers, Larry Blackmon with Cameo, Billy "Shoes" Johnson with Frankie Beverly and Maze, Tony Thompson with Chic, Zoro with Bobby Brown, and Sheila E. with Prince. House music evolved out of disco, an ultimate studio creation for the clubs with god-like quarter-note bass drums working dancers into a frenzy.

Acid jazz, also known as rare groove, came out of England and Germany around 1988, and merged soul, funk, hip-hop, and jazz. Bands like Brand New Heavies (with drummer Jan Kinkaid), Incognito (Frank Tontoh), The Young Disciples, Galliano, and US3 merged their funk with the talents of playful hip-hop artists (Guru's *Jazzmatazz*).

Funk drummers that are carrying the banner forward in the new millennium include Russell Batiste Jr. (Funky Meters, Porter, Batiste & Stoltz, Papa Grows Funk) and Terrence Higgins (Dirty Dozen Brass Band) from New Orleans, "Li'l" John Roberts, Michael Bland, and John Blackwell Jr. with Prince, and Jamal Thomas with former JB horn man Maceo Parker. All these players are continually redefining the grooves, enriching the funk for all of us.

Joseph "Zigaboo" Modeliste, of New Orleans funk institution The Meters. Zig's deep groove, unique beats, and tasty hi-hat work deeply influenced every great funk drummer who followed him.

Lissa Wales

Slingerland set it originally came with.

Regardless of how old, beat-up, or rickety a drummer's stool is, it's still his THRONE. Yeah, like a king's (or queen's) throne.

It's where royalty sits, and demands respect.

Of course, a great drummer is a benevolent dictator, leading by example, not by force. Taking fast, decisive action. Representing the people (his bandmates) with strength, grace, intelligence—and hopefully a little humor.

All hail the drummer, perched on his throne.

# Punk Rock

by Jon Wurster

By the mid 1970s, bands like Emerson, Lake & Palmer, Yes, and Rush had raised rock's technical proficiency bar to such heights that many young musicians had resigned themselves to the notion that rock 'n' roll could only ever be a spectator sport.

Punk rock changed all that.

The Descendents' Bill Stevenson,
dean of punk rock drumming

The Sex Pistols' Paul Cook

Though its roots can be traced to late–'60s/early-'70s bands like The Stooges, MC5, Dictators, and New York Dolls, it was the release of The Ramones' 1976 self-titled debut album that served as punk's ignition switch. The antithesis of the day's album-oriented rock, New York's Ramones stripped rock 'n' roll back to its absolute basics. The band's songs were short, raw, fast, and devoid of solos, and at their heart was drummer Tommy Ramone's incredibly basic 4/4 thump, which would serve as the blueprint for punk rock drummers everywhere.

The Ramones' influence spread worldwide. It was especially felt in the UK, where bored kids with little or no musical training picked up instruments and formed their own groups. Among the leading lights of the English punk scene were The Damned, The Sex Pistols, and The Clash, three bands that defined punk's in-your-face sound and attitude and featured three of the genre's most notable drummers: Rat Scabies, Paul Cook, and Nicholas "Topper" Headon, respectively.

Though firmly entrenched in punk rock, each of these drummers brought their own distinctive style to their bands. Scabies (real name: Chris Millar) propelled The

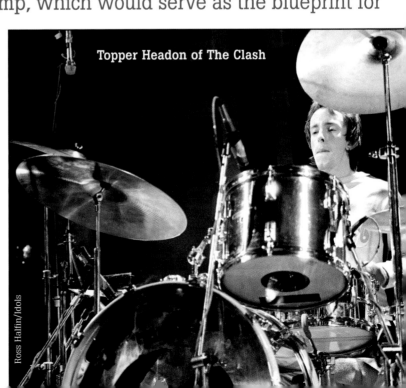

Topper Headon of The Clash

Rat Scabies of The Damned, channeling the spirit of Keith Moon

Damned with a manic, cymbal-heavy attack that was punk's closest approximation to The Who's Keith Moon, while Cook took a more controlled, no-frills approach, laying down a solid yet exciting foundation evidenced on The Pistols' lone studio album, *Never Mind The Bollocks, Here's The Sex Pistols*.

Explosive yet incredibly musical and with a background in R&B, Headon was debatably the best drummer to come out of the UK punk scene, and he played a crucial role in helping The Clash expand its musical horizons while still retaining its bite. Headon's performance on the band's landmark 1979 LP, *London Calling*, stands as one of rock's greatest.

# HARDCORE

One of punk's most important and influential offshoots was hardcore. Birthed in the US by such late-'70s bands as Dead Kennedys, D.O.A., Bad Brains, and Black Flag, and propagated by such early '80s bands as The Circle Jerks, Minor Threat, MDC, and Agnostic Front, hardcore upped punk's ante in terms of aggression, speed, and lyrical vitriol. This was intense, go-for-the-throat punk rock taken to its most extreme.

If ever there was a hardcore drum legend, it would have to be Chuck Biscuits, who in addition to being the spark plug behind Vancouver, Canada's D.O.A., also lent his considerable wallop to Black Flag, Circle Jerks, and later, hard rockers Danzig and Social Distortion.

Earl Hudson's performance on Bad Brains' 1983 *Rock For Light* LP shows a drummer remarkably adept at not only blazing hardcore but laid-back reggae as well. Bill Stevenson, a master of the lightening-fast sixteen-stroke roll, drummed for both Black Flag and The Descendents, a band whose blend of hard-driving punk and melodic pop would leave an indelible mark on many of today's biggest-selling artists, such as Blink-182, Foo Fighters, and Sum 41.

# World Music

by Martin Patmos

The ever-imaginative Airto Moreira playing a sonic sculpture. Airto initially came to prominence with Miles Davis at the very end of the '60s, and continued to spin remarkable percussive textures with foundational fusion supergroups Return To Forever and Weather Report.

**World music is a vast term, encompassing styles of music from every continent on which people have lived. And in every culture that has evolved, the power of a drum has been discovered in one form or another.**

**Whether built with a wood, clay, or metal shell, with a head of cow, goat, fish, or some other skin, drums have accompanied song and dance for centuries, beating out countless rhythms.**

## A COMPLETELY NEW DRUMMING LANGUAGE

Reggae holds a special place in the world music scene. Originating in Jamaica, it is a music of righteousness and protest, with ties to the Rastafarian religion. It is also a roots music unlike others in that it evolved after the drumset was created. In reggae, the drums play a defining role, with an original groove that is not adapted from other percussion instruments.

Sly Dunbar, reggae master

Most people's first exposure to reggae is through the music of Bob Marley. From there the music of his contemporaries and those that followed, as well as the ska music that preceded reggae, reveals a whole stylistic approach. At the heart of the style is the one-drop, with its laid-back, light groove, rhythmic emphasis on upbeats, and solid bass drum on 2 and 4 to ground things.

The one-drop originated in the early 1960s at the hands of Lloyd Knibbs with The Skatalites, and continued with Carlton Barrett's work with Bob Marley in the later 1960s. Beginning in the 1970s, Sly Dunbar arguably became the first-call reggae drummer, playing with practically every big reggae star, including Peter Tosh, Culture, Dennis Brown, and Black Uhuru. Other important drummers were Winston Grennan, who played with Jimmy Cliff, and Toots & the Maytals' Jah Bunny, who worked with dub poet Linton Kwesi Johnson. Elder statesman Leroy "Horsemouth" Wallace has had a long relationship with the great Burning Spear, and Stevie Nesbitt grooved Steel Pulse into the charts. In the hugely influential style of dub reggae, genius engineers such as Mad Professor manipulated the drums of players like Sinclair Seales to heavy psychedelic effect.

As in rock and the blues, reggae drummers continue to evolve in different directions, some re-examining its roots, and others seeking new territory. But at the heart of it all is a solid bass drum and sharp snare set off by an upbeat hi-hat, keeping the rhythm flowing.

**Martin Patmos**

Indian multi-percussion great Trilok Gurtu works with a totally unique setup that allows him to play four-limb "drumset" rhythms while squatting on the floor, without the benefit of a drum stool. Gurtu's cross-cultural playing can stun unsuspecting witnesses to his pan-global fusion.

Coming down through time, frame drums...drums shaped like hourglasses, barrels, cylinders, and cones...drums with single and double heads...and drums played with hands and sticks have been carried across the globe as populations shifted.

Although it's only been around for about a century, the drumset itself can be viewed as an instrument of world music. Looking back at the earliest trap sets, we see that it descends from Turkish cymbals, European marching drums, and Chinese tom-toms. It has become central to much of American music, and through pop, rock, and jazz has spread back to the rest of the world. Drumsets can now be found keeping the beat in music from South America, the Caribbean, Africa, Asia, and Europe. And while drumsets were first manufactured in the US, today companies making drums, cymbals, and all manner of other percussion instruments are found throughout the world.

Peruvian-born drummer Alex Acuña came to prominence in the legendary world-fusion group Weather Report. Known for his encyclopedic knowledge of ethnic rhythms, Acuña has put his exotic stamp on hundreds of albums.

Generally speaking, those styles included under the term "world music" derive from the folk music of a particular area. As folk music, many styles often don't move beyond their original instrumentation, including whatever indigenous percussion they might use.

Yet some of these folk music styles have adapted to include modern instrumentation, merged with pop and rock influences, or morphed into new styles of music altogether, as with African music styles such as juju. Where the drumset really comes into play, though, is when it draws on the percussion traditions of folk music styles, absorbing them and fitting the rhythms to its own design.

The first traces of what would become world music can be found in jazz, when Dizzy Gillespie brought Chano Pozo into his band on congas in 1947. This, along with the craze for mambos and cha-chas by Latin dance bands in the 1950s, brought Afro-Cuban rhythms to the attention of a great many musicians. It wasn't long before the infectious rhythms heard on timbales, congas, and cowbells were adapted to the drumset. And while drummers were learning and incorporating these rhythms into their styles, some Latin percussionists, such as Willie Bobo, learned to play the drumset.

Since that time an important Latin-jazz tradition has been forged, including rhythms from Cuba, Brazil, and elsewhere in the Caribbean and South America. And just as many jazz musicians were influenced and inspired by these forms, these rhythms found their way into rock too. Michael Shrieve's drumming with Santana at the end of the 1960s and into the 1970s effectively brought the Latin vocabulary to a whole new audience. Meanwhile, Latin influences were felt in funk music as well, as with the band War. And as jazz and rock came together around 1970 in fusion, both Weather Report and the early incarnation of Return To Forever had an underlying world music current due to the drumming of Brazilian Airto Moreira.

During the late 1960s, both rock and jazz were influenced by music from other cultures, most notably those of India and West Africa. While the drumset wasn't impacted right away, Ravi Shankar's tabla player, Alla Rakha, certainly turned heads, as did Babatunde Olatunji's West African–styled ensemble. Not long after this, the sound of reggae was slowly introduced to the world from Jamaica, offering a new rhythm and style.

By the dawn of the 1980s, a wealth of rhythms and styles from around the world had reached far from their origins to new audiences. And moving into the 1990s with the introduction of the CD, this universe of music became more obtainable and affordable for the curious listener. With all of this information available, many musicians experimented with mixing styles in every possible way. Mickey Hart of The Grateful Dead brought together percussionists from around the world for his Planet Drum project. Jazz was blended not just with Latin American rhythms, but musical ideas from elsewhere, as Royal Hartigan showed at times in Fred Ho's explosive Afro-Asian Ensemble. Jewish Klezmer influences found new expression in John Zorn's Masada, with Joey Baron on drums. Meanwhile, a revolving door of drummers and percussionists worked with the likes of Bill Laswell and Jah Wobble in creating world/ethnic/ambient/funk/fusion projects.

From these diverse paths have come a great number

**"IT'S A SPIRITUAL VIBE THAT I TRY TO GET FROM MY DRUMS TO THE MUSIC. BECAUSE DRUMS COME FROM THE SLAVERY DAYS AND FROM AFRICA, IT COMES FROM A LOT OF HISTORY."**
**—CARLTON BARRETT**

of drummers, playing in traditional and hybrid styles. Today's scene is loaded with talented players, such as Trilok Gurtu, who mixes classical Indian percussion ideas with elements of the drumset. Satoshi Takeishi works in a similar way, but from a Japanese perspective. Meanwhile, Manu Katché has mixed groove and world music ideas with Peter Gabriel and the Afro-pop of Youssou N'Dour, while free jazz drummer Susie Ibarra has grown by exploring gamelan and her Philippine cultural roots. There are also numerous percussionists working with rhythms and instruments from around the globe, such as Nana Vasconcelos and Mino Cinelu.

The drumset is an extremely adaptable instrument, with the ability to not only create endless rhythms of its own, but to re-create the rhythms of other percussion instruments. Sometimes tradition is respected, with just the percussive voicing altered, while other times ideas are blended, leading to new ideas.

While all the styles that make up world music move in and out of popularity, their cumulative effect on drumming is great. Meanwhile, there are styles that have yet to reach their full potential on the drumset, such as some of the popular African music styles, which still make heavy use of traditional percussion, as well as some Asian genres. With so many styles of music in the world, and so many rhythms, the potential for future grooves and new drumset ideas is remarkably exciting.

**World-class drummer Mino Cinelu combines the timelessness of ancient rhythms with the most cutting-edge electronic drum technology.**

# Unearthing World Beats

by Martin Patmos

There are so many places to begin exploring world drumming, looking for an entry point can be daunting. Perhaps the best way is to just pick a point of interest and follow it. Such an attitude can foster a sense of exploration as new music and ideas are discovered. The book *Drumming At The Edge Of Magic* by Grateful Dead drummer Mickey Hart captures this spirit of adventure well.

Recordings are probably the easiest way to appreciate world beats. A good library may have some treasures in its catalog, and a well-stocked CD store ought to have something too. There are some recordings that are duds, but if you're willing to take some risks (and if your local music store has listening stations), some great music can be discovered. There are lots of resources to help in seeking out new music too, from informational Web sites to in-depth books on particular subjects. Paying attention to the record labels

of favorite recordings can also be helpful. Some college and public radio stations have shows that feature world music, which can be instructive too.

Of course, nothing beats attending a live performance. World music performers of every stripe tour internationally, and regional and college venue listings could turn up anything. While seeking them out may involve some travel, the rewards may well be worth the effort.

For those who like to travel, the WOMAD (World Of Music Arts And Dance) festival presents a diverse collection of music from around the world, as well as international food, arts, crafts, and so forth, usually over a weekend. Originally brought about through Peter Gabriel's interests, it takes place in the

UK each year. WOMAD festivals take place internationally as well, in places like Australia, Spain, and Singapore. The festival even toured the US one summer. Such notable drummers as Billy Cobham and Manu Katché have played the event, as well as a host of other top drummers and percussionists. In bringing music from around the world to an international audience, WOMAD creates a unique experience, exposing and introducing cultures to each other.

Whether from West Africa, North India, the Middle East, or South America, world beats are endless in their variety, and waiting to be heard.

# Hands On!

## A DIFFERENT KIND OF SWEAT

by David Licht

"It can't get much better than this," I thought as I blistered my way through a wild medley of tunes with the band Shockabilly. In Shockabilly we took tunes by Jimi Hendrix, Willie Nelson, The Byrds, Roger Miller, The Beatles, Tammy Wynette, The Doors, and Thelonious Monk and chopped and blended them together to create a pretty unusual sound. (Psychedelic comedy?) The trio pushed my ability as a drummer, and my drumkit had to

produces three distinct tones: a deep bass center, a full open note near the edge, and a "pa-ta" flat-handed slap as an accent. Precise accompanying drum parts were essential to assure my place in the classes.

On one occasion I was very fortunate to have had Ladji Camara sub for Djoniba—my first "trance drumming" experience. ("Papa" Ladji Camara, lead drummer for The Guinea Ballet in the Mandingo tradition, traveled with

changed the notes, producing "open and closed" effects. Any focus on the snare drum center allowed the rest of the kit to *breathe*. Rimshots on all of the drums expanded their range as well—and kept sound engineers on their toes!

The cymbals were the icing on the cake, and became almost a separate entity. The tonal world of hammered brass is practically endless, and by using sticks, mallets, and brushes, entire songs could be played "up top." With the addition of my two feet operating pedals that made very low (bass drum) and high (hi-hat)

## AFTER EXPLORING THE WORLD OF HAND DRUMMING, I RETURNED TO THE DRUMKIT WITH A PIONEERING SENSIBILITY.

cover a lot of sonic ground. Unfortunately the band imploded after a fast four years. Still, Shockabilly's demise brought me to New York City, where one day, while I was on my way to a Brazilian batucada session (samba school) rehearsing for the annual Greenwich Village Halloween parade, I unexpectedly walked through an African dance class with live drumming. I almost froze in my tracks!

Now, I had had some experience playing conga drums back home in North Carolina in the mid '70s. I had even recorded an all-percussion album called *Paws* around 1980 with my brother Dennis, a blessed memory. And I remembered seeing an amazing Haitian drummer with The Trinidad Folk Ensemble around 1975, which was perhaps the first time I ever observed a solo hand drummer fuel an entire dance troupe. But the sheer power of this experience stuck in my head as something I could really explore someday.

In October of 1985, I was ready to take the next step. I traded a couple of snare drums for a Malian (West African) djembe drum, and I began playing for a dance class taught by Djoniba Mouflet, a master drummer from Martinique. For the next two years, three times a week, I studied in his drum class—with *lots* of practice at home between classes.

Now, djembe is played right at the center of the body, near the solar plexus, which is a high energy center—kind of like a junction box where the rest of the body can draw upon its power. Hands on this goat-skinned wonder

Katherine Dunham's dance groups in the US in the '60s. Today he's considered the father of a thriving "rhythm nation.") All of the background "support" drummers had to lock in together in order to free up the lead "solo" drummer, who in turn propelled the dancers. One angry glance was enough to tighten your part, as a second glance usually meant, Sit out!

Sometime during my first six months of study, I discovered a new focus for my drumset playing. Sitting back at the kit, I realized how many more sounds were in front of me. The tom-toms had a new meaning when I used the entire head. Pressing with the sticks

sounds, often independent of what the sticks were doing on the upper part of the kit, I had transformed into *two* drummers.

After exploring the world of hand drumming, where I really just scratched the surface in this age of global access, I returned to the drumkit with a pioneering sensibility. Blessed to be the drummer for a couple of groundbreaking bands over the years (Bongwater, The Klezmatics), I was able to view the previously limited trapkit (from the word "contraption") as a mini-orchestra of sorts, each sound working separately and together, one song at a time, from a whisper to a roar.

Macioce

# NEW WAVE

by Jon Wurster

In the late '70s and early '80s, new wave, a term coined by Sire Records head Seymour Stein in 1977, became a default tag for artists who took the spirit and energy of punk and branched out with it in myriad, often danceable directions. An astonishingly diverse group of artists fell under the new wave banner, from '60s-inspired pop bands like The Go-Go's and Blondie, to ska revivalists The Specials and The English Beat, to quirky guitar rockers XTC and Elvis Costello & The Attractions, to the just left-enough-of-center rock of The Police, The Cars, and The Pretenders, to the arty, out-there sounds of Devo, The Residents, and The B-52's.

As with punk, new wave had a "no rules" credo that extended to drumming. Whereas a drummer in a hard rock band might use his bass and snare drums to propel a song, a new wave drummer might use the hi-hat or ride cymbal bell to accomplish the same goal. New wave drummers, for the most part, seemed to favor small four- or five-piece drumkits—a rebellion against the major hard rock and heavy metal bands of the day. Needless to say, there were no double bass drums or gongs for these guys.

It's hard to overstate Police drummer Stewart Copeland's influence on the '80s drum landscape. Intricate hi-hat work, the infusion of reggae-based, off-kilter, polyrhythmic beats in a pop song context, and a tightly tuned kit helped make Copeland a distinctive percussive voice in an era of over-blown, arena-shaking drums. Copeland, an anomaly in the new wave scene in that he favored a large kit featuring multiple tom-toms and cymbals, used the extra trappings only when he wanted to add color to a song. His performance on The Police's 1979 hit "Message In A Bottle" is a perfect example of his ability to segue effortlessly from a reggae-influenced groove to full-on rock.

Perhaps no other musician of the past thirty years has made more records as disparate-sounding as Elvis Costello, and drummer Pete Thomas has been with him nearly every step of the way. Since Costello's 1977 debut album, *My Aim Is True*, he's touched on everything from amphetamine-charged rock, to Stax/Volt soul, to country & western. Check out the manic, syncopated runaway train rhythm of the 1978 single "Lipstick Vogue" and Costello's '81 cover of the country ballad "Good Year For The Roses" for proof that Thomas could handle just about anything the singer threw at him. Thomas still plays with Costello and has been an in-demand session drummer, working with Sheryl Crow, Los Lobos, and Johnny

The Pretenders' Martin Chambers. His intro to "Middle Of The Road," from the band's Learning To Crawl album, is one of the most exciting drum intros to grace a hit song.

Cash, among others.

Combining a formidable wallop with Keith Moon-style flair, Blondie's Clem Burke was new wave's premier drum showman. Though he could often be seen twirling or tossing his sticks, Burke's showmanship never got in the way of his emphatic, tom-heavy drumming style, best evidenced on the band's 1978 hit "Dreaming." Burke's colorful Premier kit, which featured an oversize rack tom and cymbals positioned flat, was as visually striking to look at as his drumming was to listen to. Burke went on to drum for Bob Dylan, Eurythmics, and The Romantics before Blondie re-formed in 1998.

Though Scotland's Big Country enjoyed only a brief period in the limelight (with the 1983 hits "In A Big Country" and "Fields Of Fire"), drummer Mark Brzezicki was hailed as one of that era's greats. Like The Police's Copeland, Brzezicki played a large multi-drum setup and favored the "traditional" stick grip. A key element of Brzezicki's unique sound was his use of marching band–inspired snare drum rolls, a device that heightened the anthemic qualities of Big Country's soaring, guitar-driven songs. Brzezicki later recorded with The Who's Pete Townshend and Roger Daltrey.

One of the biggest-selling records of 1982 was The Go-Go's' *Beauty And The Beat*, an album loaded with incredibly catchy, danceable rock anchored by drummer Gina Schock's authoritative backbeat. Schock was one of new wave's most physical drummers, an avowed John Bonham disciple who boasted a formidable right foot of her own. Schock served as a role model for a generation of young female drummers who had yet to really have one. Her non-stop pumping on The Go-Go's' 1981 hit "(We Got) The Beat" is one of the era's most enduring drum performances.

Stewart Copeland of The Police. His influence would be difficult to overestimate.

Paul Natkin/Poto Reserve

**BLONDIE'S CLEM BURKE WAS NEW WAVE'S ULTIMATE DRUM SHOWMAN. HIS COLORFUL PREMIER KIT, WHICH FEATURED AN OVERSIZE RACK TOM AND CYMBALS POSITIONED FLAT, WAS AS VISUALLY STRIKING TO LOOK AT AS HIS DRUMMING WAS TO LISTEN TO.**

Rick Malkin

Among many other accomplishments, Terry Bozzio designed electronic drumkits, such as the one he's playing here with Missing Persons.

Ebet Roberts

U2's Larry Mullen Jr. Mullen's military-like snare drum intro to "Sunday Bloody Sunday," from the band's third album, *War*, represents one of the most identifiable drumming "hooks" in popular music history.

Gina Schock of The Go-Go's: Working out her Bonham fixation.

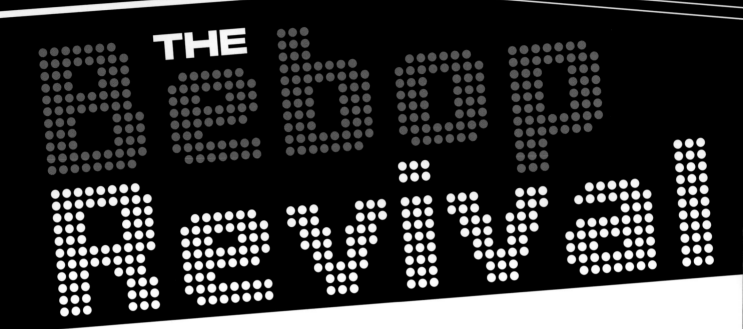

# THE Bebop Revival

by Michael Dawson

The 1970s were turbulent times for jazz. While jazz-rock fusion was embraced among the decade's rock 'n' roll generation, the audience for acoustic straight-ahead jazz was dwindling. Miles Davis, one of the genre's most innovative figures, even discarded the style, labeling it "the music of the museum."

Jazz drummers during this time period were faced with either adapting to the changes in the music (which mainly involved the incorporation of rock/R&B grooves and free jazz concepts) or staying true to their bebop roots. Most chose to adapt.

Art Blakey and his Jazz Messengers, with Wynton Marsalis, Charles Fambrough, and Branford Marsalis

Drummers Tony Williams and Jack DeJohnette originally made their mark in the post-bop of the 1960s, but also became forerunners of fusion drumming. After leaving Miles Davis's quintet, Tony formed his cutting-edge jazz/rock trio Lifetime. His drumming with Lifetime, which was a clear departure from his post-bop style of the '60s, was a major influence on an entire generation of fusion drummers.

DeJohnette, whose unconventional playing appeared on Miles' groundbreaking *Bitches Brew*, recorded many cross-genre albums throughout the 1970s. He also became active as a bandleader, releasing a variety of records for German jazz label ECM. His bands Compost, Directions, New Directions, and Special Edition incorporated elements of rock, pop, free jazz, and mainstream jazz into an esoteric blend that defies categorization. The drummer would return to acoustic jazz in the 1980s, as a member of pianist Keith Jarrett's Standards Trio.

Bebop originator Max Roach also reinvented himself in the 1970s. He embraced the avant-garde on a series of duet records with saxophonists Anthony Braxton (*Birth And Rebirth*) and Archie Shepp (*Long March*), and with pianist Cecil Taylor (*Historic Concerts*). He also formed his landmark percussion ensemble M'Boom during this time.

Karega Kofi Moyo

**Famoudou Don Moye, of The Art Ensemble Of Chicago, was a major influence during the '70s avant-garde movement.**

M'Boom, which featured Roach, Warren Smith, Freddie Waits, Omar Clay, Joe Chambers, Roy Brooks, and Ray Mantilla, recorded their debut recording, *Re: Percussion*, in 1973.

While many of his peers chose to modify their drumming during the tumultuous '70s, hard bop pioneer Art Blakey stood his ground. The energetic drummer refused to stray from the swinging, acoustic jazz sound that he helped create in the '50s with his band The Jazz Messengers. And by the end of the 1970s, his perseverance paid off.

In 1979, Art Blakey heard teenage trumpet prodigy Wynton Marsalis and invited the young musician to join his band. Wynton eventually joined The Jazz Messengers in 1980 and quickly became the figurehead of a youthful bebop revival. After only one year with Blakey, nineteen-year-old Marsalis left the Messengers to embark on a hugely successful solo career.

For his debut, Wynton Marsalis chose to use two rhythm sections. One consisted of members from Miles Davis's legendary '60s quintet: bassist Ron Carter, pianist Herbie Hancock, and drummer Tony Williams. The other featured a collection of Wynton's peers: bassists Charles Fambrough (of The Jazz Messengers) and Clarence Seay, pianist Kenny Kirkland, and then–unknown drummer Jeff "Tain" Watts. These up & coming "young lions" played a major role in a rebirth of acoustic jazz in the 1980s.

Because of his affiliation with Marsalis, Jeff Watts was at the forefront of jazz drumming during the bebop revival. Ironically, Tain's drumming reflects less bebop influence than that of his peers. His background was in classical percussion, R&B, and fusion. It wasn't until the drummer attended the Berklee College Of Music that he began studying straight-ahead jazz. As a result, Tain stood out among the majority of his peers with a unique brand of bebop/fusion drumming that would be highly influential on many jazz drummers who emerged in the 1990s.

Jack DeJohnette: a vital link between
many jazz drumming styles.

But Watts' approach (which emphasized originality over traditionalism) was not the norm during the bebop reawakening of the late '70s and early '80s. This was an era when drummers were steeped in jazz history, and often based their playing on the vocabulary of bebop masters Max Roach, Philly Joe Jones, Art Blakey, Elvin Jones, and Tony Williams. Some of these bebop revivalists included Kenny Washington, Carl Allen, and Lewis Nash.

Nash is one of the most highly regarded drummers of the '80s bebop revival. His crisp, post-bop style made him a first-call sideman for hundreds of jazz sessions. Nash's first prominent gig was with vocalist Betty Carter in 1981. The drummer would appear on many of Carter's recordings, including 1988's Grammy-winning disc *Look What I Got*. Nash also performed and recorded with other modern jazz giants, including pianists Tommy Flanagan, Oscar Peterson, and McCoy Tyner and tenor saxophonists Sonny Rollins and Joe Henderson.

Nash has also been closely associated with younger musicians of the '90s neo-bop generation, appearing on recordings with saxophonist Antonio Hart, trumpeter Roy Hargrove, and bassist Christian McBride. He's played for vocalists Diana Krall, Natalie Cole, and Jane Monheit as well.

Like many of his peers, drummer Marvin "Smitty" Smith began his career as a sideman to older jazz stars. In 1981, he recorded *Love* with legendary vocalist Jon Hendrix. He also appeared on *Gumbo* and *Jewel* with saxophonist Bobby Watson in '83.

But Smith was not only interested in traditional jazz. While he continued to work with a variety of straight-ahead jazz artists, the drummer also took on projects that challenged the bebop purism of the time. In 1984, the drummer delved into the avant-garde on adventurous saxophonist David Murray's *Children*. That same year, Smith joined bassist Dave Holland's unconventional fusion/jazz ensemble.

While in The Dave Holland Quintet, Smith incorporated elements of funk, fusion, post-bop, and free jazz into each performance. Smith's multi-faceted drumming is best documented on the quintet's discs *Seeds Of Time* and *The Razor's Edge*.

Smith also developed a close relationship with one of his bandmates, forward-thinking saxophonist Steve Coleman. Coleman's unprecedented concepts for improvised music, which became known as M-BASE (Macro–Basic Array of Structured Extemporizations), helped establish a fresh, urban-influenced sound that would greatly impact the future of jazz. Smith appears on several of Coleman's discs, including the saxophonist's 1985 debut, *Motherland*.

From his early days on New York City's vibrant jazz scene to his long-held seat with the Tonight Show band, Marvin "Smitty" Smith is one of the most versatile drummers working today.

## ESSENTIAL LISTENING

**Jack Dejohnette**
**Special Edition**
(Jack DeJohnette)

**Art Blakey And The Jazz Messengers**
**Album Of The Year**
(Art Blakey)

**Wynton Marsalis**
**Black Codes (From The Underground)**
(Jeff "Tain" Watts)

**Tommy Flanagan**
**Jazz Poet**
(Kenny Washington)

**Freddie Hubbard with Woody Shaw**
**Double Take**
(Carl Allen)

**Tom Harrell Quintet**
**Moon Alley**
(Ralph Peterson)

**John Scofield Trio**
**Out Like A Light**
(Adam Nussbaum)

**Woody Shaw**
**Stepping Stones: Live At The Village Vanguard**
(Victor Lewis)
**Night Music**
(Tony Reedus)

**Ray Brown Trio**
**Bass Face**
(Jeff Hamilton)

**Mulgrew Miller**
**Keys To The City**
(Marvin "Smitty" Smith)

**Joe Lovano Quartets**
**Live At The Village Vanguard**
(Lewis Nash and Billy Hart)

# Post-Punk

by Jon Wurster

A number of bands that formed in punk's wake rejected the melodic, sometimes cheery sensibilities of the new wave groups, taking cues instead from earlier innovators like The Velvet Underground, Television, Kraftwerk, and Suicide. "Post-punk" bands like Joy Division, Siouxsie & The Banshees, Echo & The Bunnymen, and The Cure embraced a sound that was dark and complex. Many of the genre's drummers incorporated drum machines, samplers, and exotic percussion into their playing to achieve the desired moods and textures.

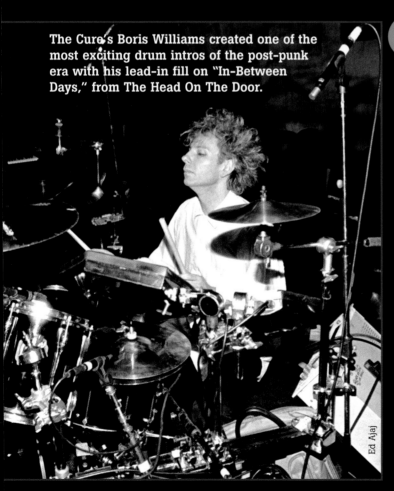

The Cure's Boris Williams created one of the most exciting drum intros of the post-punk era with his lead-in fill on "In-Between Days," from The Head On The Door.

Ed Ajaj

Formed during London's punk explosion and featuring Sex Pistol Sid Vicious as their first drummer, Siouxsie & The Banshees proved to be one of the more adventurous and longest-surviving of the class of 1976 bands. Peter "Budgie" Clarke may not have played on the band's first two albums, but he will forever be known as the definitive Banshees drummer. By the time the Banshees called it a day in 1996, Budgie had provided the rhythmic backbone for ten of the band's studio releases—albums that found him drawing from a varied percussive palette that included innovative tom-tom/snare drum interplay ("Happy House" from 1980's *Kaleidoscope*), tricky hi-hat off-beats ("The Sweetest Pill" from '85's *Tinderbox*), and marimba ("Swimming Horses," off '84's *Hyaena*).

Liverpool's Echo & The Bunnymen made a wise decision in 1979 when they replaced their drum machine and namesake, "Echo," with flesh-and-blood drummer Pete de Freitas. De Freitas added a muscular punch to the band's swirling, psychedelic music, an approach best evidenced by his galloping tom-tom pounding on "Back Of Love" from the Bunnymen's '83 album, *Porcupine*. When a more somber vibe was required, De Freitas often opted to use brushes instead of drumsticks, as he did on the 1983 single "The Killing Moon." Though he died tragically in a 1989 motorcycle accident, de Freitas' unique style continues to influence new generations of drummers.

Though known early on for its gloomy, gothic dirges, the

NEW ORDER'S STEPHEN MORRIS FORGED AN EDGY, ROBOTIC DRUM STYLE THAT MADE LISTENERS QUESTION WHETHER OR NOT THEY WERE IN FACT HEARING A MACHINE AND NOT A HUMAN DRUMMER.

**Budgie of Siouxsie & The Banshees: innovative snare/tom work, hi-hat offbeats.**

London-based Cure developed a tender, more accessible side that would take them straight to the high reaches of the pop charts in the late '80s. Boris Williams may have been just one of four Cure drummers, but he was the man behind the kit for the band's biggest hits: "In Between Days," "Just Like Heaven," and "Friday, I'm In Love." One of Williams' key assets was his ability to contribute whatever was needed to help give The Cure's songs the perfect vibe, from the simple, straight-up, driving drum pattern of 1985's rollicking "In Between Days," to the swirling cymbals and dirge-like snare drum pounding found on "Plainsong," the lead-off track on the band's '89 album, *Disintegration*. Williams could also affect a song's feel by using different drum tunings, as with the taught, popping snare sound featured on the funky "Hot Hot Hot" from '87's *Kiss Me, Kiss Me, Kiss Me*.

Few post-punk bands have had as lasting an influence as Manchester, England's Joy Division and its post–Ian Curtis incarnation, New Order. Formed in 1977, Joy Division personified post-punk's gloomy, emotive, often sterile sound. Drummer Stephen Morris played a crucial role in forging this sound with his edgy, robotic drum style—check out "Isolation," from the band's 1980 album, *Closer*—that made the listener question whether or not they were in fact hearing a machine and not a human drum-

mer. When lead vocalist Curtis committed suicide in May of 1980, Morris and his surviving Joy Division bandmates formed New Order, a pioneering electronic/club group that actually *did* rely heavily on drum machines (often mixed with Morris's acoustic drumkit). New Order's '83 smash, "Blue Monday," featuring a Morris-programmed, thumping, bass drum–heavy beat, went on to become the biggest-selling 12" dance single in history.

## RECOMMENDED LISTENING

**Joy Division**
**Closer** (Stephen Morris)

**Siouxsie & The Banshees**
**JuJu** (Budgie)

**Public Image Limited**
**Public Image** (Jim Walker)

**Magazine**
**Real Life** (Martin Jackson)

**Killing Joke**
**Killing Joke** (Paul Ferguson)

**Pere Ubu**
**The Modern Dance** (Scott Krauss)

**Wire**
**On Returning (1977-1979)**
(Robert Gotobed)

**The Fall**
**Grotesque (After The Gramme)**
(Karl Burns/Mike Leigh)

**The Cure**
**The Head On The Door** (Boris Williams)

**Gang Of Four**
**Entertainment** (Hugo Burnham)

**Bauhaus**
**In The Flat Field** (Kevin Haskins)

**Birthday Party**
**Prayers On Fire** (Phil Calvert)

**Tears For Fears**
**Songs From The Big Chair**
(Manny Elias)

**Echo & The Bunnymen**
**Ocean Rain** (Pete de Freitas)

# Alternative

R.E.M.'s Bill Berry: part of the whole

The mid to late '80s was a time of great creativity and growth in the world of underground, non-commercial rock 'n' roll. Record bins teemed with vinyl from artists influenced not only by punk and its aftershocks, but also by everything from the challenging sounds of Captain Beefheart and Can to the decidedly uncool '70s schlock of The Defranco Family and KISS. While mainstream media initially shied away from the likes of X, The Pixies, Sonic Youth, The Replacements, and Camper Van Beethoven, these bands were embraced wholeheartedly by a network of college radio stations and fanzine writers who helped spread the word.

# Rock

by Jon Wurster

Though there is little stylistically to link many of the bands or drummers that flourished during this period, most did share an ethos that placed creativity over commercialism. A handful of these artists, like R.E.M., Red Hot Chili Peppers, and The Smiths, would go on to achieve massive world-wide success. Others, like Hüsker Dü, The Minutemen, The Replacements, and Fugazi would have to settle for "legendary" or "seminal" status.

The music made by these bands was a direct precursor to the Nirvana-led alternative rock explosion of the 1990s, as well as a source of inspiration for many of the indie rock bands like Pavement, Superchunk, and Sebadoh that flourished during the same period.

R.E.M.'s Bill Berry understood perfectly that drums are only one piece of a greater musical puzzle. A large part of the Athens, Georgia band's initial appeal was the way the four members' instruments and voices weaved together to create a unique fabric of sound, without any of its individual components attracting undue attention. The band's 1983 debut album, *Murmur,* showcases Berry's ability to not only "hold down the fort" with an economical four-on-the floor beat ("Sitting Still"), but also to come up with incredibly intricate bass/snare/hi-hat interplay ("9-9"). R.E.M. scored huge hits in the early '90s with *Out Of Time* and *Automatic For The People,* two albums featuring songs co-written by the drummer. Berry left R.E.M. in 1997.

Key players in Los Angeles' burgeoning late-'70s punk scene, X went on to evolve into a top-notch rock band during the '80s by incorporating elements of rockabilly, folk, and country into a unique sound. Don "DJ" Bonebrake, a classically trained percussionist who could also whack the drums with maximum force, hit upon the perfect balance of raging rock power and subtle musicality. One of Bonebrake's greatest performances comes during "The Hungry Wolf," the lead-off track on the band's 1982 album, *Under The Big Black Sun,* where he brilliantly maneuvers from a pummeling Bo Diddly floor-tom beat to a tricky tom/bass drum/snare polyrhythm and then into a raging punk gallop. Bonebrake also performed with The Knitters, a country/folk X-spinoff band that allowed the drummer to show off his impressive brush skills.

Steeped in guitar dissonance as well as free jazz and punk rock, New York's Sonic Youth were one of the most influential groups of '80s underground rock. When drummer Steve Shelley joined the band in 1985, he brought with him a penchant for the same kind of hypnotic, chugging tom-tom rhythms that drummer Maureen Tucker had employed with The Velvet Underground, as well as a propensity for experimentation. A trademark of Shelley's unique style is his use of maracas, mallets, and shakers in tandem with his drumkit, to achieve a driving sound despite the avoidance of cymbals. One listen to "Teenage Riot" from the band's '87 album, *Daydream Nation,* is all the proof one needs that Shelley can also bash out straight rock 'n' roll with the best of them.

It's almost impossible to come up with a succinct description of the music of San Pedro, California's Minutemen. Over the course of the band's brief five-year run (1980-85), The Minutemen released a torrent of records touching on such seemingly incongruous genres as punk, country, funk, jazz, and acoustic folk. Somehow, drummer George Hurley was able to shift between these styles as if each was second-nature to him. *Double Nickels On The Dime*, a 1984 two-LP set, is both the band's and Hurley's crowning achievement. From the funky opening salvo of "Anxious Mo-Fo," to the rapid-fire snare rolling on "This Ain't No Picnic," to the square dance two-step of "Corona" (a song that would find a worldwide audience some sixteen years later as the theme to the TV show *Jackass*), Hurley's drum tracks comprise the perfect foundation for an album many view as one of the most important in '80s alternative rock.

Dirk Vandenberg

**The Minutemen's George Hurley: blending the incongruous**

# Digressions Of A STAND-UP

Karen Keene

**Victor DeLorenzo takes an unexpected break from his role as stand-up drummer with beloved alternative buskers Violent Femmes.**

When I started to play drumset some thirty-odd years ago, I never thought that someday I'd be standing up to earn my living as a professional drummer. At that time, all the drummers that I admired sat down behind their collections of wood and metal to guide and power some of the most exciting bands in my ever-expanding musical universe.

My favorites included such diverse talents as Tony Williams, Elvin Jones, Ed Blackwell, Ringo Starr, Keith Moon, Hal Blaine, Roy Haynes, Charles Moffit, Carl Palmer, Jo Jones, Sunny Murray, Don Moye, Levon Helm, and so many more masters of time and taste. The only time these fellows would stand up behind their drumsets was to either set up or tear down. I had only heard the term "stand up" applied to comedians or to describe someone's character as a fine law-abiding person. Drummers didn't stand up to perform. They played music sitting down! It wasn't allowed, or so I thought at the time….

Then along came my introduction to the music of The Velvet Underground and the gender-bender earth crushing drumming of one Maureen (Mo) Tucker. She played fierce driving beats on a snare drum, batter-side-turned-up bass drum, and big cymbals, usually with the aid of mallets instead of sticks. Although she used such an unorthodox setup, she played with a conviction that never let you think for a second there was something lacking in the drum department. Mo's playing was peppered with a very adventurous freedom, a primitive growl that whipped and slashed through melody and lyric. Her drums and her style gave me something that every young drummer has to realize. "Economy Is King!" Oh, and yes…She was STANDING UP!

All this not only made sense to me musically, but the stand-up bit fed the reason for my entrance into showbiz in the first accursed place…. I finally had some bread for my ham acting.

When the three of us started Violent Femmes, we wanted a musical outfit that was as portable as it was powerful—something that traveled well. I usually just had some kind of snare drum (I wasn't that particular in my early punk rock days), a stand, and a pair of brushes. All this fit nicely in a fiber snare drum case. The equipment situation wasn't hard to figure out. What challenged me was how to create or imply phantom drumset figures and sounds with just a pair of brushes and one lonely snare. But whether this could work with my acoustic bass guitar–playing partner was the haunting question. We had played drumset and electric bass together many times quite successfully, but I wondered if we could have a big sound with so little.

Hmmm…what could I do to help myself? I knew that I wanted the snare drum to sing so the metal brushes could activate many different areas of the top and bottom head, the rims, and sometimes the drum shell. This tuning approach went right against the prevalent taped-up, dead drum sound of early-'80s rock. But I couldn't worry about fitting in with all of that. I needed the drum to ring so I could do my thing.

Now, the standing-up bit was an entirely different performance problem. I liked the flashy idea of not being tethered to a specific drumset realm, but by standing up, I also saw the distinct picture of trouble I would have trying to play any kind of hi-hat or bass drum. I wasn't quite sure how my ankles would take the weight and the strain, so I decided to try to make the "single drum theory" work first. I figured that later on I could worry about breaking my feet for the sake of music. So for now, a snare drum and brushes would be my drumset. Now I was free to think about not only how to put the music across with such a tiny drum system, but how I could interpret the comedy and drama that was/is Violent Femmes music.

# DRUMMER

Since I had worked on the stage since childhood as an actor, the other guys and I decided to exploit my extroverted style. I knew how to draw attention to myself as a performer, but I was also equipped to give stage focus to my musical partners at any given time for effect and enhancement of the music. We decided that my little drum world would exist downstage center at the lip of the stage. This was, and still is, a very atypical stage position for a modern drummer to occupy. But we weren't going for a normal approach. I wanted to be "the Keith Moon of stand-up comedy drumming" and then some....

I still find it funny when I arrive at the venue before the evening's show and hear the stage crew asking where the rest of the drums are. Then after the show, I'm very proud that the same crew was amazed that I'd been able to get a big, full sound from so little. I've worked extremely hard over the years to consistently pull off this magic trick. And it's not done with any mirrors, believe me....

Over the years I've used many different setups, depending on what was called for by our ever-evolving music. I've even used a homemade device called a Tranceaphone, which is a floor tom mounted on a snare stand, covered by a metal bushel basket. When played with metal brushes, it produces a "ping" sound that reminds me of a very bad cymbal that someone else might throw in the garbage. I like to try and make something

musical out of something that's considered trash. It pushes one's mind to hear the musical beauty that exists in all things around us. God bless John Cage and Marcel Duchamp!

During the course of the many hours, months, and years that have added up to this thing called a career, I've been most happy and flattered by the way our fans have stuck by me through all my different drum phases. So many musicians don't have the luxury of being accepted and encouraged to redefine their perceived normal patterns of musical behavior. I relish my position, I'm thankful for it, and I'm happy to report that I'm still standing.

The band that launched a thousand—make that *ten* thousand alternative bands: The Velvet Underground, featuring Maureen Tucker on stand-up drums.

## RECOMMENDED LISTENING

**R.E.M.**
Murmur (Bill Berry)

**Replacements**
Let It Be (Chris Mars)

**Minutemen**
Double Nickels
On The Dime
(George Hurley)

**Red Hot
Chili Peppers**
The Uplift Mofo
Party Plan
(Jack Irons)

**Julian Cope**
Saint Julian
(Chris Witten)

**Dinosaur Jr.**
You're Living
All Over Me
(Murph)

**Fishbone**
Truth And Soul (Fish)

**Butthole Surfers**
Locust Abortion
Technician
(King Coffey and
Theresa Taylor)

**Pixies**
Surfer Rosa
(David Lovering)

**Robyn
Hitchcock
& The Egyptians**
Element Of Light
(Morris Windsor)

**The Smiths**
The Queen Is Dead
(Mike Joyce)

**Mudhoney**
Mudhoney
(Dan Peters)

**Fugazi**
13 Songs
(Brendan Canty)

**Let's Active**
Afoot/Cypress
(Sara Romweber)

**Hüsker Dü**
Zen Arcade
(Grant Hart)

**Camper Van
Beethoven**
Camper Van
Beethoven
(Chris Pedersen)

**Sonic Youth**
Daydream Nation
(Steve Shelley)

**Mission Of
Burma**
Mission Of Burma
(Peter Prescott)

**X**
Under The
Big Black Sun
(D.J. Bonebrake)

The Red Hot Chili Peppers dig in hard, as drummer Chad Smith lays down one slamming punk-funk groove after another.

Jay Blakesberg

ROCK

by Adam Budofsky

**L**ike every sub-style of rock 'n' roll, the modern rock movement of the late '80s/early '90s simultaneously refuted and honored the sounds that came before it. The logical extension of the punk/new wave/alternative rock evolution, modern rock was explicitly interested in being loud, aggressive, and

Aldo Mauro

anti-establishment. But it also turned the clock back in many ways, harking back to the medium tempos, complex arrangements, and sonic colors of classic rock bands, especially Led Zeppelin, as well as the slippery grooves of funk groups like Sly & The Family Stone and Parliament-Funkadelic. The drummers who came out during this period had to incorporate many years of rock innovations. The ones who made a lasting impression were those who stamped their own personality on the music.

Stephen Perkins of Jane's Addiction, Porno For Pyros, and his own improv-based band, Banyan, extended the role of the drums in modern rock with his tribal, linear grooves.

# PRIMUS'S SOUND WAS ALL ABOUT RHYTHM AND HUMOR, AND TIM ALEXANDER KNEW HOW TO HIGHLIGHT BOTH ASPECTS BRILLIANTLY.

Around 1987, an unusual band from New York named Living Colour began to make headlines with their funky, riff- and solo-laced rock that featured a punk-like energy and blazingly sharp technique. Living Colour's African-American lineup didn't go unnoticed, though since many of rock's architects were black—Little Richard, Chuck Berry, Jimi Hendrix—that fact really shouldn't have been such a headline-maker. No matter. Drummer Will Calhoun gleefully basked in the band's whirlwind of influences, which included Zeppelin, P-Funk, and hardcore-reggae heroes Bad Brains. Calhoun's formidable technique, including round-house fills and deft footwork, was allowed to shine brightly in the live arena and on the quartet's albums. As such,

Calhoun helped set the tone for many hot young rockers who would make their name in the ensuing years.

Bay Area band Primus, featuring the skewed vocals and monster bass work of Les Claypool, provided a different but equally fascinating array of ideas for drummer Tim Alexander to explore. An amalgam of styles that really shouldn't have worked—largely Zappa, Rush, and post-punk—Primus's sound was all about rhythm and humor, and Alexander knew how to highlight both aspects brilliantly. The drummer's work on the band's hit "My Name Is Mud" features his tell-tale flappy gong drum/bass drum combos and gutter groove.

Many of modern rock's biggest names would find large, sympa-

Living Colour's Will Calhoun. After cutting his teeth with Caribbean superstar Harry Belafonte, he helped usher in a powerful new modern-rock drum vibe: muscular, rhythmically sophisticated, and dynamic.

thetic audiences on the famous Lollapalooza tours, which were the brainchild of singer Perry Farrell of the influential LA band Jane's Addiction. Jane's was the first post–classic rock group to blatantly conjure the ghost of Led Zeppelin, though that wasn't the limit of their appeal. In Stephen Perkins, Jane's had a flamboyant, searching player who in time would find many clever ways to orchestrate complex patterns around his kit. By the time Perkins played *Modern Drummer* magazine's Festival weekend in 1996, his setup featured various hand drums and unusual cymbals, which he used to elicit hypnotic, tribal beats. Perkins' approach can be heard clearly on the hit song "Pets" by the Jane's spin-off band Porno For Pyros, and on improvisations with his band Banyan.

The longest-running and most successful band associated with modern rock is The Red Hot Chili Peppers. After releasing a string of albums that showed increasing promise, the band vaulted to international fame with the Rick Rubin–produced *Blood Sugar Sex Magik*. Finally coming up with the perfect rock/funk recipe, The Chili Peppers stormed the charts with several hit singles, and inspired hordes of bands influenced by their combination of

styles, which include rap, old-school funk, and classic LA punk rock. Previously slowed by a revolving drum chair, which had included Jack Irons (later of 11 and Pearl Jam), the band found a keeper in Chad Smith, whose personality fit immediately with the outrageous, fun-loving band. More importantly, Smith's understanding of ghost-note-laden funk beats, and his internalization of the classic rock blueprints of Zeppelin's John Bonham and Deep Purple's Ian Paice, made him the perfect musical match. Smith understood how to support and individualize the group's multi-faceted hits, such as the hard funker "Give It Away," the rolling 12/8 of "Breaking The Girl," and the ballad "Under The Bridge." The Red Hot Chili Peppers' hot streak continues today.

Variations on the Chili Peppers' funk-rock sound would find success with a number of popular '90s bands. Many of these groups featured drummers who were highly influential in their own right, such as Mike Bordin with hard-hitters Faith No More, Chad Sexton with the reggae-loving 311, Brad Wilk with profoundly important rap-metal pioneers Rage Against The Machine, and Adrian Young with multi-platinum hit makers No Doubt.

Unique among their peers were Chicago's Smashing Pumpkins,

# JIMMY CHAMBERLIN'S DRAMATIC CHOPS, PLAYED OUT ON A EXTENDED, OUT-OF-ORDE DRUMKIT, DID MUCH TO ATTRACT DRUMMER EAGER TO DISSECT HIS PARTS.

Gene Ambo

Michelle Martin-Coyne

# STEVEN DROZD IS THOUGHT BY MANY MODERN-ROCK AFICIONADOS TO BE THE REINCARNATION OF JOHN BONHAM, LAYING DOWN THE JUICIEST, MOST SOULFUL GROOVES THIS SIDE OF THE '70S

featuring the burning, fusoid drumming of Jimmy Chamberlin. The Pumpkins didn't show much interest in the day's overwhelming influence of rap, focusing instead on grand proggish gestures, goth-rock atmospherics, and a huge, appealing wall-of-guitar sound. Chamberlin made a statement from the get-go, as his silky snare fills on their 1991 debut album, *Gish*, betrayed an almost Buddy Rich–like approach. Chamberlin's dramatic chops,

One of the surprising success stories of the '90s was The Flaming Lips, a garage-psych band out of Norman, Oklahoma who matured into one of the most entertaining, exploratory, and tuneful bands of its generation. Drummer Steven Drozd is thought by many modern-rock aficionados to be the reincarnation of John Bonham, laying down the juiciest, most soulful grooves this side of the '70s. After surviving the fallout from a novelty hit ("She

Brad Wilk of Rage Against The Machine and Audioslave. Heavy, detailed, and massively grooving.

Alex Solca

played out on a extended, out-of-order drumkit, did much to attract drummers eager to dissect his parts, and the band enjoyed a string of hit albums until their sound would somewhat fall out of favor. Against the odds, Chamberlin again made drumming headlines in 2005 with a mostly instrumental solo outing by his group The Complex.

Don't Use Jelly"), The Lips went on to release several highly regarded albums, such as 1999's *The Soft Bulletin*. Besides being a drop-dead mammoth drummer, Drozd is an active songwriter with The Lips, and plays most of the keyboards and guitars on their albums, making him a true renaissance musician.

Other drummers who made their mark in the mid- to late-'90s were The Black Crowes' Steve Gorman, Cindy Blackman with Lenny Kravitz, Stone Temple Pilots' Eric Kretz, Adam Wade with Jawbox and Shudder To Think, Andy Sturmer with Jellyfish, Jeff Buckley's Matt Johnson, Ween's Claude Coleman, Billy Conway and Jerome Deupree with Morphine, A Perfect Circle's Josh Freese (who would go on to become his generation's Steve Gadd), Live's Chad Gracey, Dave Grohl's Foo Fighters bandmate Taylor Hawkins, William Goldsmith of revered emo architects Sunny Day Real Estate and The Fire Theft, and perennial favorite Carter Beauford with The Dave Matthews Band. Beauford in particular became a major drum hero in the late '90s due to his slippery hi-hat approach, metronomic time, and highly complex groove ideas, which appealed to an entire generation who hungered for the technical mastery of '70s funk and fusion,

Cindy Blackman, who initially gained notoriety as the flashy live drummer with Lenny Kravitz, is also an accomplished jazz player with heavy supporting credits and several releases as a leader.

Carter Beauford of The Dave Matthews Band brought a busy, broken-up '70s groove to the air-waves in the late '90s.

but played by a band who understood the jam-band ethic of the '90s.

Many of the most fascinating drummers of the early twenty-first century are players whose influence extends well past the drum stool, and into the areas of composition and sound manipula-tion. Among the players who will likely help sound the charge of drummer-as-multi-tasker are Sebastian Thomson with Trans Am, Glenn Kotche with Wilco, Ben Massarella, Brian Deck, and Jo Adamik with the Chicago-area collective Califone, Dodo Nkishi with Mouse On Mars, Michael Lowry with Lake Trout, Jon Theodore with The Mars Volta, Jojo Mayer with his band Nerve, and Zach Hill with Hella.

Hill is the most shocking of all of these players, spewing out a torrent of non-stop hand/foot ideas, which in the studio he manipulates with all means of distortion. The result is a power-fully disorienting sound that nearly overwhelms with its barrage of ideas. Upon repeated plays, though, strange patterns begin to emerge, and listeners begin to understand the method. It's just this sort of demanding conceptual approach that breathes life into modern rhythmic pursuits, and promises to keep future drumming conversations very lively indeed.

The Mars Volta

# 5 Rock Futurists

**Jojo Mayer** (Nerve)
**Zach Hill** (Hella, Team Sleep)
**Jon Theodore** (The Mars Volta)
**Glenn Kotche** (Wilco)
**Virgil Donati** (Planet X)

# MANY OF THE MOST FASCINATING DRUMMERS OF THE EARLY TWENTY-FIRST CENTURY ARE PLAYERS WHOSE INFLUENCE EXTENDS WELL PAST THE DRUM STOOL.

Shannon Clifton

Zach Hill of Hella, Nervous Cop, and Team Sleep. Startling hand-foot combinations, endless stamina, and copious distortion make his performances some of the most unnerving and refreshing in modern music.

Susan Nielsen

Though his tenure in the band would be prematurely cut off, Dave Abbruzzese made a lasting impact with his emotional and precise drumming in Pearl Jam. Young drummers especially had an affinity for Abbruzzese, whose inviting personality resulted in many a player being delighted by an up-close encounter with their hero.

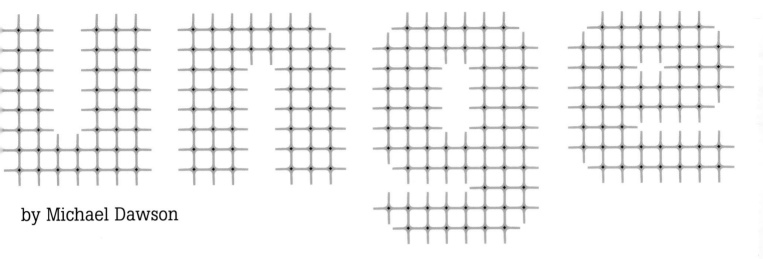

by Michael Dawson

In 1991, alternative rock announced its arrival to mainstream America when a powerhouse trio from Aberdeen, Washington known as Nirvana invaded the homes of the *MTV*-obsessed with their anti-rock anthem "Smells Like Teen Spirit." This unexpected hit, from the band's major-label debut, *Nevermind*, was exactly what legions of Generation-Xers were waiting for. Its pungent blend of hardcore punk energy and brilliant songwriting provided much-needed relief from the self-indulgent hair metal and super-smooth pop that was dominating the airwaves.

At the core of Nirvana's intoxicating sound (which was a combination of the mid-tempo sludge rock of The Melvins, the soft/loud dynamics of The Pixies, and the melodic prowess of The Beatles) was a hard-hitting rhythm section of bassist Chris Novoselic and monster drummer Dave Grohl, who had previously served time with legendary D.C. punk outfit Scream. Grohl, who joined the band shortly before recording *Nevermind*, made his presence known with an earth-shattering snare/kick entrance to "Smells Like Teen Spirit," followed by some of the most impassioned and expertly crafted drum performances in modern rock history. With the help of Grohl, *Nevermind* became a success, symbolically knocking "King Of Pop" Michael Jackson from the top of the charts in 1991.

In the wake of Nirvana's meteoric rise, the local alternative rock scene in Seattle, Washington quickly became the focal point of the entire music industry. While bands like The Melvins, with highly influential drummer Dale Crover, and Green River, with drummer Alex Vincent, pioneered the gritty punk-meets-metal Seattle sound in the 1980s, the alt-rock genre now known as

"grunge" is largely linked to Nirvana and three of their peers—Soundgarden, Alice In Chains, and Pearl Jam.

Soundgarden was the first Seattle-based alternative band to sign to a major record label. Their 1989 A&M release *Louder Than Love* marked the beginning of a growing interest in the underground rock sounds that were coming out of the Pacific Northwest. But it wasn't until the release of *Badmotorfinger* in 1991 and a subsequent opening slot on LA rockers Guns N' Roses' *Use Your Illusion* tour that Soundgarden, with their Led Zeppelin / Black Sabbath-inspired brand of grunge rock, began to receive widespread national exposure.

Soundgarden's drummer, Matt Cameron, shared with Grohl a passion for high-energy performances and natural drum sounds. But his unique style is more improvised, reflecting a jazz and fusion influence. Cameron favors darker cymbal sounds and smaller drums, and his drumming is full of subtlety. On the band's first semi-hit, "Outshined," Cameron fills out the song's odd-timed grooves with ghost-notes, hi-hat rolls, and offbeat fills. On "Jesus Christ Pose," he sets up a complex tom-based pattern beneath the band's dissonant guitar lines and chainsaw riffs.

Another Seattle grunge band, Alice In Chains, with rock-solid drummer Sean Kinney, also helped pave the way prior to Nirvana's global breakthrough. The dark and gloomy Sabbath-influenced sound of their 1990 debut, *Facelift*, was sopped up by heavy metal and post-punk fans alike. And with the help of a hit video for the poignant track "Man In The Box" and tours with Van Halen, Poison, and Iggy Pop, Alice In Chains eventually earned a gold record, becoming grunge's first major success story. Their follow-up album, *Dirt*, was released in 1992 during the peak of the grunge rock explosion. Key performances from Kinney include *Facelift*'s "Man In The Box," *Dirt*'s "Would," and "No Excuses" from Alice In Chains' 1994 acoustic EP, *Jar Of Flies*.

**Dale Crover of the inimitable Melvins. Sludgy tempos, huge drums, and an idiosyncratic approach to classic-rock beats define Crover's gargantuan drum performances.**

Shaun Brackbill

When grunge originators Green River disbanded in 1988, two of its members, singer Mark Arm and guitarist Steve Turner, along with drummer Dan Peters, formed garage rockers Mudhoney, who became one of Seattle's most influential bands after signing to famed independent record label Sub Pop. The remaining members, guitarist Stone Gossard and bassist Jeff Ament, created Mother Love Bone, a melodic hard rock band that broke away from the Black Flag / Black Sabbath roots of their peers in favor of blues-based sounds of Led Zeppelin, Jimi Hendrix, and early '70s groups like Aerosmith and Free.

Mother Love Bone went on to sign a major-label deal with Polydor. But when frontman Andrew Wood died of an overdose in 1990, the Gossard/Ament duo banded together to create grunge's most commercially successful outfit, Pearl Jam. But before they did that, Stone and Jeff joined with Soundgarden's Chris Cornell and Matt Cameron to record a tribute to Wood, titled *Temple Of The Dog*. This release introduced the world to Pearl Jam's new singer, Eddie Vedder, who shared vocal duties on the single "Hunger Strike." The album also foreshadowed a later reunion in which Cameron would take over drum duties for Pearl Jam in 1998.

The drum seat in Pearl Jam has been as tumultuous as the history of the band itself. Matt Cameron drummed on the band's original demos, but his commitment to Soundgarden prevented him from joining full-time. Local Seattle drummer Dave Krusen took over before the recording of *Ten*. Krusen's loose, jazz-inspired groove was a major part of the success of this breakthrough album, but he left the band shortly after its release to battle his addiction to alcohol. Then Edie Brickel's rising star drummer, Matt Chamberlain, stepped in for a six-week period (which included the filming of the video for the single "Alive") before heading off to NYC to join the *Saturday Night Live* band. Thankfully, before heading east, Chamberlain recommended an energetic drummer from Dallas, Texas for the gig.

Dave Abbruzzese joined Pearl Jam just in time to record two tracks for the soundtrack to the 1992 grunge-centric film *Singles*. His performance on the song "State Of Love And Trust" is a perfect introduction to the drummer's slippery rock feel and super-tight snare sound, as well as his penchant for splash cymbal accents, hi-hat flourishes, and ghost note–laden grooves. Abbruzzese also appeared on Pearl Jam's classic *MTV Unplugged* performance in March of '92, 1993's follow-up record *Vs.*, and part of 1994's *Vitalogy*.

Abbruzzese may have been the most visible and highly regarded of Pearl Jam's drummers, but by the time they went into the studio to record *Vitalogy*, relations between drummer and band turned sour. So Abbruzzese was dismissed. Longtime friend and alternative rock veteran Jack Irons (Red Hot Chili Peppers, Eleven) accepted an invitation to complete the sessions. Irons remained with Pearl Jam through two additional studio releases (*No Code* and *Yield*) and a collaborative effort with grunge godfather Neil Young (*Mirror Ball*) before leaving the band abruptly in 1998 for health reasons. Matt Cameron then returned to the band, completing several world tours, recording 2000's *Binaural*, and appearing in the concert DVD *Touring Band 2000*.

Although plagued with internal turmoil throughout their career, Pearl Jam remains the only mainstream grunge band to have survived the decade. Nirvana came to a screeching halt after singer/guitarist Kurt Cobain committed suicide in '94, Soundgarden disbanded in '97 to pursue other interests, and Alice In Chains slowly dissolved into oblivion after their haunting performance on *MTV Unplugged* in '96.

Matt Cameron, expert at smoothing out the rough edges around odd time signatures. Soundgarden hits such as "Outshined," "Black Hole Sun," and "Spoonman" all featured deviations from rock's standard 4/4 beat.

Starfile

## "I LIKE TO FEEL THAT SONGS ARE LIKE ROLLING GEARS IN AN ENGINE, THAT EVERYTHING CLICKS IN THE PATTERNS, AND PIECES OF THE GEAR MEET AT CERTAIN TIMES AND THEN DISAPPEAR, EVENTUALLY COMING BACK TOGETHER AGAIN."
### –DAVE GROHL

Paul La Raia

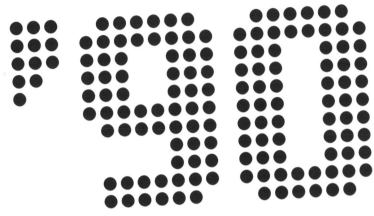

# '90s

by Michael Dawson

## The early 1990s was a fruitful period for all genres of music.

Alternative rock had taken over mainstream radio, hip-hop's audience was growing rapidly, and, thanks to its resurgence in the early-1980s, acoustic bebop-influenced jazz was continuing to gain popularity among a younger generation of listeners. In response to this rising interest, record labels scrambled to sign a variety of new jazz artists who embodied the youthful spirit of the time.

These "New Young Lions," like their predecessors in the '80s, were deeply rooted in jazz history. They favored tight hardbop-styled arrangements and high-energy improvisations. And they often revisited standard jazz repertoire. But this new generation of jazz musicians also drew influence from the 1960s post-bop of Miles Davis and John Coltrane, the free-form interplay of Ornette Coleman, and the modern pop/rock sounds of The Beatles and James Brown. The resulting combination of classic bebop virtuosity, the adventurous spirit of '60s post-bop and free jazz, and contemporary musical concepts (such as odd time signatures, syncopated funk grooves, and asymmetrical forms) created a new, exciting, and commercially viable brand of mainstream jazz.

For drummers of this era, the demands were high. Not only were they expected to have a deep understanding of the traditional jazz vocabulary of bebop masters Max Roach, Philly Joe Jones, and Art Blakey. They also had to have a handle on the rhythmic complexities of modern masters Tony Williams, Elvin Jones, Roy Haynes, and Jack DeJohnette, while also being able to lay down a funky Clyde Stubblefied-inspired groove.

**Modern jazz icon Jeff "Tain" Watts:
Jack of all trades, master of each and every one.**

BO-BOP

100 Years Of Rhythmic Power And Invention  ⋮  **THE DRUMMER 151**

One of the most prominent drummers of this time was Jeff "Tain" Watts. While his groundbreaking work with trumpet virtuoso Wynton Marsalis is often linked to the bebop revival of the 1980s, his drumming with saxophonists Branford Marsalis, Kenny Garrett, and Michael Brecker in the late-'80s and early '90s helped establish a new approach to modern jazz drumming. Whether laying down odd-time grooves ("Bullworth" from Brandford's *Requiem*), steamrolling through an up-tempo burner ("2 Down & 1 Across" from Garrett's *Songbook*), or exploring free-form textures ("The Beautiful Ones Are Not Yet Born" from Branford's *The Beautiful Ones…*), Watts found the perfect balance between convention and innovation, thus setting the groundwork for the neo-bop era.

Another highly influential drummer, Bill Stewart, rose to widespread acclaim in the early '90s. Stewart's landmark performance on guitarist John Scofield's 1990 release *Meant To Be* showcased the drummer's unique assimilation of the masters, including the crystal-clear phrasing of Miles-era Tony Williams, the snap-crackle 'comping of Roy Haynes, and the melodicism of Ed Blackwell. Stewart also incorporated a highly interactive hi-hat foot and

Bill Stewart is a hot property among jazz elite.

Ebet Roberts

## TAIN TRACKS

**Branford Marsalis**
The Beautiful Ones Are Not Yet Born
The Dark Keys
Requiem

**Michael Brecker**
Two Blocks From The Edge

**Kenny Garrett**
Songbook

## STEWART'S SELECTS

**John Scofield**
Meant To Be
What We Do
Hand Jive

**Maceo Parker**
Mo' Roots

**Pat Metheny**
Trio 99>00

## BLADE'S BEST

**Kenny Garrett**
Triology
Pursuance: The Music Of John Coltrane

**Joshua Redman**
Spirit Of The Moment
Freedom In The Groove
Timeless Tales (For Changing Times)

## NEO-BOP ESSENTIALS

**Joey Baron**
John Scofield
Grace Under Pressure

**Greg Hutchinson**
Joe Henderson
Lush Life: The Music
Of Billy Strayhorn

**Clarence Penn**
Makoto Ozone
Trio

**Adonis Rose**
Nicholas Payton
Payton's Place

**Jorge Rossy**
Brad Mehldau
The Art Of The Trio,
Vol. 3: Songs

**Matt Wilson**
Dewey Redman
In London

**Billy Drummond**
Billy Drummond
Dubai

Brian Blade's playing on Joshua Redman's Live At The Village Vanguard became a blueprint for a generation of late-'90s neo-boppers.

polyrhythmic phrasing into the mix. The drummer also showed off his soulful side at the start of the '90s, touring and recording several discs with funk master saxophonist Maceo Parker.

Two years later, in 1992, the jazz world was introduced to another major drumming force, Brian Blade, on saxophonist Kenny Garrett's *Black Hope*. Blade's emotionally charged drumming echoes the passion and unpredictability of Elvin Jones, the deep swing of Philly Joe Jones, and the creativity of Tony Williams, while also incorporating unerring musical instincts and

supreme dynamic control. He would also appear on Garrett's *Triology* and *Pursuance: The Music Of John Coltrane*, and he was a regular member of acclaimed saxophonist Joshua Redman's group. Blade also drummed on Norah Jones' Grammy-winning *Come Away With Me* and is a member of jazz legend Wayne Shorter's award-winning quartet.

Other drummers who came to prominence during the '90s neo-bop movement include Gregory Hutchinson, Clarence Penn, Adonis Rose, Jorge Rossy, Joey Baron, Billy Drummond, and Matt Wilson.

The New...

Atom Willard has logged many musical miles with Rocket From The Crypt, The Offspring, Moth, and Weezer drummer Patrick Wilson's side project, The Special Goodness. Willard hits hard—very hard—and sets the tone for unshakable precision and raging emotion in each setting.

# PUNK

by Waleed Rashidi

In the fall of 1991, after a decade below the radar, punk rock finally broke through the mainstream—and it hasn't veered off course since. That year, Seattle's Nirvana, featuring drummer Dave Grohl, topped the commercial charts with its major-label debut, *Nevermind*. In addition to launching the grunge movement, Nirvana's wildly successful, melody-laced debut instantly kicked open doors for an incredible slew of punk-based acts to follow.

A few years later, a pair of California underground punk acts took center stage: Bay Area pop-punkers Green Day, and their darker counterpart, the Orange County–based band Offspring. Featuring the drumming of Tré Cool and Ron Welty, respectively, these bands instantly treated fans to two distinct variations of contemporary punk. Whether it was Cool's loose, booming tom pattern on the breakdowns of Green Day's "Longview," or Welty's cross-sticked ticking on the intro of "Come Out And Play (Keep 'Em Separated)," 1994 arrived full of musical promise for a genre that, just a couple years earlier, was largely relegated to college radio stations, independent record stores, and small live venues.

Soon, sub-genres of the new punk scene began to splinter off, and divisions like emo-rock began to emerge. Though its roots could be traced back to the Dischord Records punk scene of the '80s (and Fugazi in the '90s), a further refined version of the sub-genre had taken form in Arizona's Jimmy Eat World, plus Midwest bands like The Get Up Kids and The Promise Ring. Though the latter two bands never saw much mainstream success, Jimmy Eat World, with drummer Zach Lind, eventually hit platinum via a string of singles from their 2001 self-titled album.

Still brewing in the underground throughout the '90s were groups like ALL and The Descendents, both featuring the highly inspirational performance, song-writing, and production skills of drummer Bill Stevenson, whose three-decade involvement in the scene played an important role in shaping current melodic punk acts. Also prevalent were the double-timed skate-punk beats played by NOFX, most notably featuring drummer Erik Sandin, whose rapid drumming on 1994's *Punk In Drublic* was one of the scene's benchmarks. The venerable Bad Religion hit with "21st Century (Digital Boy)," featuring the solid timekeeping of Bobby Schayer. And the mid-'90s start-up of snotty rockers Blink-182 eventually hit multi-platinum, as their drummer, Travis Barker, became one of rock's most famous slammers. East Coast–based melodic hardcore came into view in the '90s via Lifetime's *Hello Bastards* and *Jersey's Best Dancers* records, boasting an amazing blend of sheer power and speed, courtesy of drummer Scott Golley.

The new millennium found punk splitting in further directions. Lo-fi garage punk made its way into living room stereos by 2001 with bands like The White Stripes (with Meg White) utilizing the genre's original minimalism aesthetic to its advantage. Melodic hardcore began to proliferate and mutate with groups like Texas-based At The Drive-In (2000's *Relationship Of Command*), and more recently with Thrice, Thursday, and Taking Back Sunday. Pushing the original three-chord aesthetic even further afield, a fusion of punk, progressive rock, and classic rock met head-to-head in The Mars Volta, whose 2003 release *De-Loused In The Comatorium* featured some of punk rock's most captivating and electrifying work, courtesy of talented drummer Jon Theodore.

**Tré Cool of Green Day. His attitude may be right out of the Keith Moon/Rat Scabies school of crazed indifference, but his playing is solid as a rock.**

John Shearer/Idols

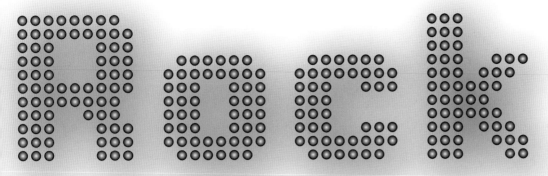

# ROCK

GREEN DAY

## NOTABLE MENTIONS

**Rocket From The Crypt** Scream Dracula Scream (Atom)

**Lagwagon** Trashed (Derrick Plourde)

**Hot Water Music** Live At The Hardback (George Rebelo)

**Fugazi** End Hits (Brendan Canty)

**Dashboard Confessional**

A Mark, A Mission, A Brand, A Scar (Mike Marsh)

**Melvins** Stag (Dale Crover)

# Jam

Bill Kreutzmann (left) and Mickey Hart of quintessential jam band The Grateful Dead. Many a Deadhead has trance-danced to the duo's infamous live "Drums" excursions.

Jay Blakesberg

# bands

by Michael Parillo

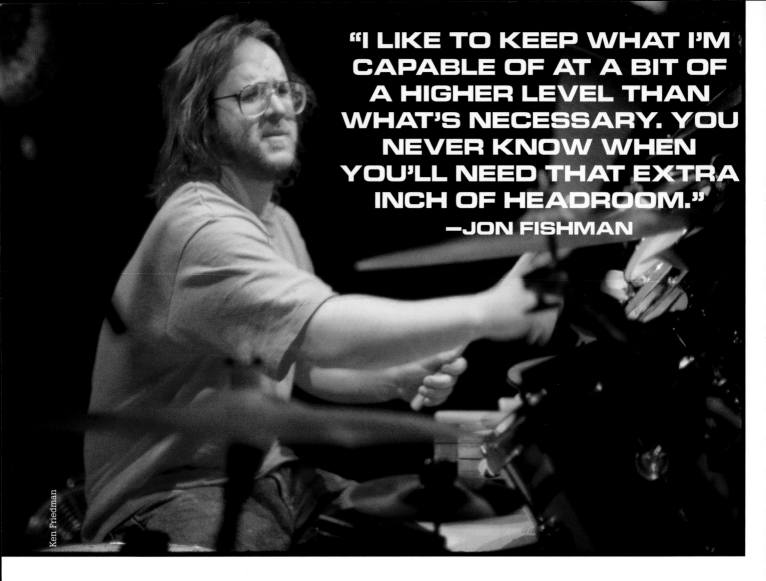

"I LIKE TO KEEP WHAT I'M CAPABLE OF AT A BIT OF A HIGHER LEVEL THAN WHAT'S NECESSARY. YOU NEVER KNOW WHEN YOU'LL NEED THAT EXTRA INCH OF HEADROOM."
—JON FISHMAN

Though it's been pretty well agreed upon that '70s-era improvisational rock groups like The Grateful Dead and The Allman Brothers are the forefathers of today's thriving jam band scene, it's tempting to widen the scope. Was Cream a jam band? Was Led Zeppelin? What about The John Coltrane Quartet? And hey, those wicked 19th-century chamber ensembles—did they start the whole thing with their violins and cellos?

Regardless of when it began, musicians jam. And if the jam is about inspiration and not precision, improvisation and not composition, the jam drummer is epitomized by The Grateful Dead tandem of Bill Kreutzmann and Mickey Hart. Kreutzmann has a light, jazzy feel, his nimble ride cymbal beat allowing the music to take flight. Hart tends to be more tom heavy, the grand gestures behind his patterns influenced by globetrotting forays into hand drumming and ethnic percussion. The two mesh beautifully yet stay out of each other's way, complementary pairs of sloshing hi-hats dripping from the ceiling and churning audiences into ecstasy. "Dark Star," on the group's first in-concert LP, 1969's *Live/Dead*, remains one of rock's great jam vehicles.

As the '70s began and The Dead worked its magic on the west coast, The Allman Brothers were jamming just as hard in the southeast, with Butch Trucks and Jaimoe Johanson leading the way. On numbers like "In Memory Of Elizabeth Reed," the drummers play as if they're of one mind and body, laying down a thick bed of ride-snare rhythm for the soloists to luxuriate

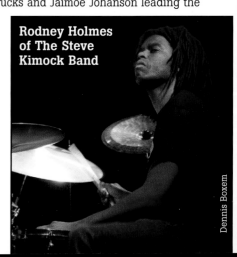

**Rodney Holmes of The Steve Kimock Band**

Butch Trucks (left) and Jaimoe Johanson of The Allman Brothers Band. The definition of complementary rhythmatists.

Starfile

upon. The Allmans brought the jam concept to new heights—and lengths—with their stretching, swinging, thirty-four-minute "Mountain Jam" on 1972's *Eat A Peach* LP.

Meanwhile, the guys who would later form Phish were paying close attention, and soon they'd make their mark. Jon Fishman, capable of training his body to perform absurd feats of coordination, is a more sensitive listener than a doctor with a stethoscope. His tireless energy, innate mastery of metric modulation, and droll wit kept his bandmates well fed with ideas, helping Phish, formed in '84, dominate the post-Dead scene of the '90s to secure a permanent place in the jam pantheon. As guitarist Trey Anastasio once told *MD*, "It's no coincidence that the band is called Phish."

Today's jam scene is a loose, all-encompassing collective defined first and foremost by the fans. Their appetite for music is insatiable, and they have no patience for bands, however talented, that shy away from taking risks onstage. Witness the Benevento/Russo Duo's explosion in popularity. In a stripped-down format that focuses on telepathic hook-ups, drummer Joe Russo seems to know his buddy Marco Benevento's next move on the keys before Marco does. Russo possesses the agility of a jazzer, the feel of a funkster, and the mind of a mad scientist. Andrew Barr of The Slip takes a more shamanistic approach, praying to the drum gods for the strength to slay dragons and move mountains with his sleek, crisp playing. He can coax a crowd into the same trancelike state that he reaches through his deep connection with his instrument and his bandmates.

Package tours and festivals, from the forward-thinking H.O.R.D.E. shows of the early '90s to the wildly diverse Bonnaroo weekends of recent years, help bands share fans and extend their influence, and continue to prove that the jam devotee doesn't care about genre and just wants to be rocked. The artists clearly agree. Kris Myers of Umphrey's McGee has a master's in jazz drumming but knows how to mash a double pedal with the power and precision of a metalhead. Rodney Holmes of The Steve Kimock Band brings

monster chops, a bright imagination, and whisper-to-roar dynamics to Kimock's stylistically ambiguous guitar-based instrumentals. And Michael Travis of The String Cheese Incident incorporates congas, bongos, timbales, and electronics into his kit as his band hops from pop to bluegrass to Dead-style explorations.

Whether or not one cares for the term "jam band"—and plenty of musicians have decried the label while nevertheless being well compensated by jam fans' money—the concept of reaching the promised land through improvisation will always run strong through rock 'n' roll. The cross-pollination and blurring of genres will continue, but the jam will remain.

## The Snare Drum

Alex Solca

From the press rolls of Baby Dodds to the backbeats of Zigaboo Modeliste, the snare drum has proven itself to be the most expressive element within the drumkit. No other drum can express so many different varying degrees of tone and dynamics as the snare. The delicate flurries in the brush work of Elvin Jones, the subtle grace notes of David Garibaldi, and the reverberant power of Bonham's 16th notes all demonstrate that the snare can embody beauty, groove, or sheer brute force with a twist of the wrist. Each element of the drumset possesses its own personality, but, as it has been said before, the snare is the heart of the kit.

**Stanton Moore**

By the mid-'80s, metal drumming had hit many forks in the road, quickly heading in a variety of directions. Some of the most notable drumming in the genre hailed from the faster-harder-louder ethic. Pushing the rock envelope at full tilt, the lightning-quick tempos of contemporary metal bands demanded previously uncharted foot speed, and the hurried hands of metal drummers made more compelling use of every piece in their increasingly large multi-tom kits.

by Waleed Rashidi

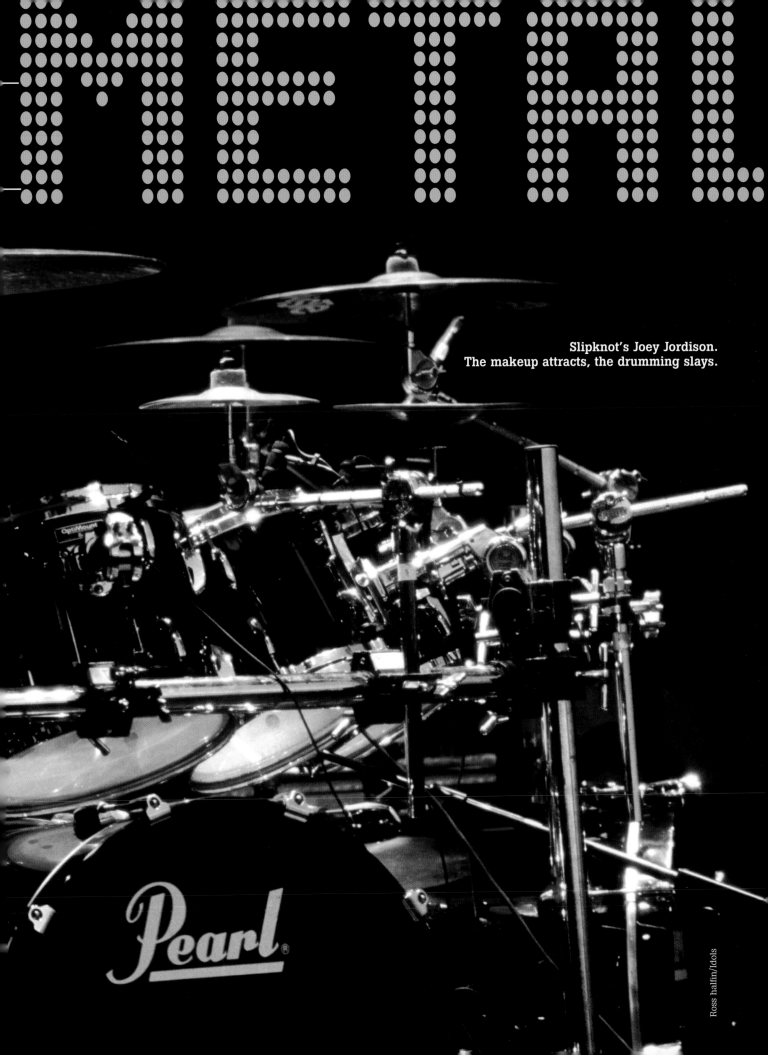

# METAL

Slipknot's Joey Jordison.
The makeup attracts, the drumming slays.

Pearl®

Ross halfin/Idols

**N**ow in their third decade, Metallica is one of today's most popular, celebrated, and important metal acts. Though they launched their career with 1983's groundbreaking *Kill 'Em All* album, the band's breakthrough came in 1986 with *Master Of Puppets*. Powered by drummer Lars Ulrich, perched behind a row of toms, Metallica's once-underground sound suddenly became commonplace. Their notoriety further increased with 1988's *...And Justice For All*, which provided Metallica with their first bona fide MTV hit in "One." Suddenly Ulrich's syncopated double kicking was all over the nation's radio waves.

Blasting off in '83 as well, Slayer pushed metal's foundation to further extremes, beginning with the rough 'n' ready debut *Show No Mercy*. Pile-driving rhythms and monumental tom runs courtesy of drummer Dave Lombardo helped the foursome's 1986 entry, *Reign In Blood*, set new standards in extreme metal. The act's following two full-lengths, 1988's *South Of Heaven* and 1990's *Seasons In The Abyss*, are also considered genre classics, again with Lombardo's relentless charge providing the propulsion behind each track.

Riding on the extreme rails from the late '80s and well into the '90s was Exodus, a thrash-metal outfit that featured John Tempesta, who also served time in three other pivotal metal acts: Testament, White Zombie, and Helmet. Pantera's famous 1992 release, *Vulgar Display Of Power*, found drummer Vinnie Paul performing with a ferocious groove previously unheard in metal.

Musical intricacies within the metal genre were stretched far with prog-metal, popularized by groups like Dream Theater. The band, which was founded in 1985, features Mike Portnoy, who became a drum hero for many, performing challenging parts with ease and more than a nod to Rush's Neil Peart. Two decades later, Portnoy and the Theater are still one of the sub-genre's most popular acts.

Banking on the heavy riffs, but juxtaposed by a decidedly funkier drum approach, was rap-metal, set into action by Anthrax's collaboration with Public Enemy on 1991's "Bring The Noise," featuring drummer Charlie Benante. Some point to an earlier collaboration between classic rockers Aerosmith and old-school rappers Run-DMC, boasting Joey Kramer's signature "Walk This Way" beat. Regardless, acts like Limp Bizkit (with drummer John Otto) led a full-flown nü-metal charge in the mid '90s. The rap-rock hybrid was also an integral part of the politi-cally charged and wildly popular Rage Against The Machine, with its edgy, driving pulse delivered by drummer Brad Wilk.

Metal simultaneously took a moody turn in the '90s, with nearly silent passages countered by blaring progressions, usually within the same song. Tool's 1993 hit single, "Sober" (from their *Undertow* album, with drummer Danny Carey) appealed to a new group of fans willing to embrace such dynamic extremes. Plowing similar territories were Deftones, whose *White Pony* found Abe Cunningham balancing all-out war on the kit with a prescribed pacifism. And rap/nü-metal front-runners Korn, with drummer David Silveria, threw their hat in the ring with the popular *Follow The Leader* album.

Stage makeup, which was all the rage in the glam-metal world of the '80s, returned in the late '90s, albeit with a decidedly macabre approach. Slipknot, with drummer Joey Jordison (a.k.a. #1), and Mudvayne, with Drummer Matt McDonough (a.k.a. sPaG, a.k.a. Spug), merged creative stage personas with overwhelming technical expertise, leaving notable live impressions. Jordison, hair flying wildly, pumps out blazing and complex patterns. Meanwhile, McDonough, whose act recently stopped wearing its signature makeup, assails the kit with blurred-stick rudiments and unpredictable bass drum patterns. Both acts prove that there's more to the genre than merely some memorable faces.

# METALLICA'S BREAK-THROUGH CAME IN 1986 WITH *MASTER OF PUPPETS.* SUDDENLY LARS ULRICH'S SYNCOPATED DOUBLE KICKING WAS ALL OVER THE NATION'S RADIO WAVES.

## NOTABLE MENTIONS

**Faith No More,** The Real Thing (Mike Bordin)

**Sepultura,** Chaos A.D. (Igor Cavalera)

**Lamb Of God,** Ashes Of The Wake (Chris Adler)

**System Of A Down,** Toxicity (John Dolmayan)

Metallica's Lars Ulrich

Jason Bittner of Shadows Fall: "I've always been recognized primarily for my ability to play two bass drums. The kick is the most important part of my sound. But I always try to play for the song."

Mike Haid

Morgan Rose of Sevendust

Slayer's Dave Lombardo

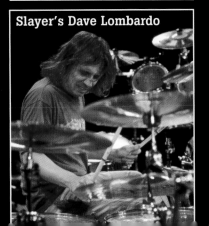

Ebet Roberts

Pantera's Vinnie Paul

Velvet Revolver's Matt Sorum

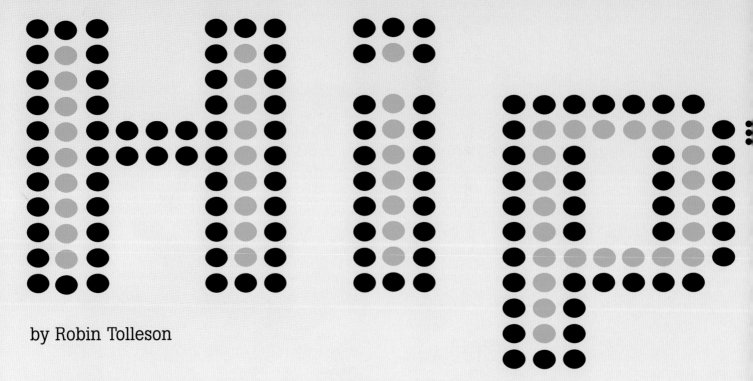

# Hi Hop:

by Robin Tolleson

Take a dose of funk, mix in a swing feel, and heavy up the backbeat. This half-time shuffle is hip-hop.

Paul La Raia

Hip-hop bands have historically been arranged musically around the DJ/turntablist, with programming, sampling, and looping a vital part of the feel and sound as well. But arguably—excuse me, Cool Herc—the best hip-hop albums being made today make use of live drummers, whether it's The Roots, where Ahmir "?uestlove" Thompson's drums lash the groove all the way through, or Black Eyed Peas, where Keith Harris puts his chops to good use on the kit around a majestic array of programmed, looped, or sampled beats.

Hip-hop, which has its roots in New York street parties during the late 1970s, quickly expanded into an entire culture. DJs like Cool Herc, Pete DJ Jones, Grandmaster Flash, and Africa Bambaataa were at ground zero in Harlem and The Bronx, overlapping and mixing their favorite grooves and breakbeats from old soul and funk records like James Brown's "Funky Drummer" and The Winstons' "Amen Brother." These DJs brought in friends to MC the parties, pump up the crowds, and keep the flow going, and their rhythmic commentary became what we now call rap.

The Sugar Hill and Enjoy labels produced the first hip-hop product. Among the earliest hip-hop drummers were Keith LeBlanc, who played on Sugar Hill Gang's "Rapper's Delight," and Emmett Nixon, who dropped serious groove on Trouble Funk's 1982 Sugar Hill release "Drop The Bomb." LeBlanc knew it was all about the dance groove, and synthetic handclaps aside, he did some interesting things doubling up on

**Ahmir "?uestlove" Thompson of The Roots. A drum scholar of the highest degree, ?uestlove is one of the most in-demand producer-players on the hip-hop scene.**

# Hop

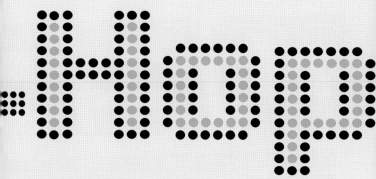

**Keith Harris of Black Eyed Peas**

Alex Solca

kick drum accents and hi-hat swing while keeping the 2 & 4 priority. Dennis Chambers became Sugar Hill's house drummer following LeBlanc, playing on Grand Master Flash's "The Message" in 1982. Even earlier, Ricky Wellman pioneered the skipping swing beat of go-go with Chuck Brown & The Soul Searchers in the late 1970s, a groove that producer Teddy Riley later mixed with hip-hop to create new jack swing. (Check out Blackstreet's "No Diggity," featuring a sample of Bill Withers' "Grandma's Hands.")

As rap became a crossover phenomenon in the early '90s, its biggest stars continued to employ live musicians when the mood hit. Cheron Moore played drumkit with hardcore rappers like Dr.

## Drum 'N' Bass
### TAKING IT TO THE EXTREME

Out of the underground DJ scene in England in the mid-1990s came the hi-energy drum 'n' bass and jungle movements, in which DJs like Goldie and LTJ Bukem sped up breakbeats to tempos in the 140-180 bpm range. Some DJs,

Heinz Krnberger

Jojo Mayer

like Roni Size and Talvin Singh, utilized live drums and upright bass along with loops and samples, and some drummers, like Jojo Mayer, Tony Verderosa, Zach Danziger, Johnny Rabb, and Yuval Gabay of Soul Coughing, simulated these outlandish breakbeats with amazing accuracy. Percussionist Karsh Kale connected electronic dance music with the sound of tabla and Indian classical music to create what he calls Asian Massive.

Dre (1991's *The Chronic*) and Snoop Dog (*Doggy Style*). The Brand New Heavies merged their funk with hip-hop artists to create *Heavy Rhyme* in 1992, with drummer Jan Kinkaid leading the charge. West coast hip-hoppers The Pharcyde have used live drummer JMD on many of their tracks since 1992. And Rasa Don

(Donald Jones) played drums on Arrested Development's "People Everyday" (1992), borrowing a slice of Sly's "Everyday People."

Later in the decade, hip-hop beats could be heard in a variety of styles, from contemporary jazz to chill/lounge settings. Rocky Bryant played all through Branford Marsalis's *Buckshot LeFonque* project in 1994. Gene Lake's awesome funk and hip-hop drumming steered Me'shell Ndegeocello's 1996 release *Peace Beyond Passion*. And Genji Siraisi powered the world funk grooves of Groove Collective on acid jazz classics like *Dance Of The Drunken Master*.

Today the trend continues. With Black Eyed Peas, Keith Harris fills the groove out around loops and samples of all varieties. And The Roots, a rare, self-contained unit of hip-hop musicians and rappers, feature drummer Ahmir "?uestlove" Thompson laying down the thickest grooves, daring a program or a loop to play heavier, flow better, or crack a better cross-stick. There's no better argument for the live hip-hop drummer than ?uestlove, who has also contributed fine playing and producing to albums by Jill Scott, Joss Stone, The Philadelphia Experiment, and D'Angelo.

Three recent releases signal a bright future for hip-hop in many forms. The Yohimbe Brothers, featuring DJ Logic, Living Colour guitarist Vernon Reid, and drummer Deantoni Parks, released *The Tao Of Yo*. The Roots' funky and gritty *The Tipping Point* continued that band's march ahead of the hip-hop curve. And hip-hop producer Madlib released *Stevie*, a tribute to Stevie Wonder played live by the Yesterdays New Quintet, featuring drummer Otis Jackson Jr. These albums and others prove that despite hip-hop's allegiance to the sample, there's much creative ground to be explored when the beats are supplied by real flesh-and-blood drummers.

# MODEF

By the end of the '90s, jazz musicians were beginning to branch further out, incorporating elements of other musical styles beyond what's traditionally labeled "jazz." The result was the creation of a variety of sub-genres that challenged the purist perspective of the bebop revival of the 1980s. Hip-hop beats, world rhythms, classical harmonies, pop-rock melodies, and free improvised avant-garde concepts all became intertwined into an eclectic mix that has created fresh and exciting new sounds for the twenty-first century.

Antonio Sanchez brings a creative approach, Latin fluidity, and blistering technique to the music of Pat Metheny and modern fusion giants.

Alex Solca

# N Jazz Fusion

by Michael Dawson

Gene Lake does it all, from out jazz to earthy funk.

Alex Solca

Jenny Bagert

**Terence Higgins of The Dirty Dozen Brass Band**

A lthough Latin music has been associated with jazz since bebop pioneer Dizzy Gillespie's landmark collaborations with conga master Chano Pozo in the 1940s, in the mid-'90s there was a crop of young Latin jazz musicians who were as influenced by modern jazz as they were by traditional Latin styles. One such musician, Mexican-born drummer Antonio Sanchez, came to prominence in 2000 when he shared drum duties with another modern fusion innovator, Jeff Ballard, on Israeli bassist Avishai Cohen's *Colors*. Sanchez's unique brand of Latin-influenced jazz drumming is technically remarkable and musically expressive, as is evident in his work with fellow Latin artists David Sanchez, Danilo Perez, and Miguel Zenón, and with modern jazz giants Michael Brecker and Pat Metheny.

Two other leading Latin jazz drummers include Adam Cruz and Dafnis Prieto. Cruz has displayed his diverse drumming skills on recordings with the Mingus Big Band, saxophonist David Sanchez, and legendary pianist Chick Corea. He's also a member of pianist Danilo Perez's adventurous post-bop trio. Prieto has appeared on equally wide-ranging projects, including discs with contemporary Latin jazz group The Caribbean Jazz Project, avant-garde trailblazer Henry Threadgill, and M-BASE saxophonist Steve Coleman.

Like Latin music, hip-hop has a history with jazz that dates back a number of years. And by the beginning of the twenty-first

THE DRUMMER : *100 Years Of Rhythmic Power And Invention*

"THERE ARE CERTAIN ELEMENTS OF FREE-DOM INVOLVED IN WHAT I DO, BUT THERE'S ALSO AN EQUAL AMOUNT OF DISCIPLINE AND FORM. I DON'T THINK IT'S EVER TOTALLY OPEN."
—NASHEET WAITS

Paul La Raia

century, drummers with strong backgrounds in R&B and hip-hop began appearing on albums with many of the era's top jazz artists.

Gene Lake is a versatile modern fusion drummer who's as adept with avant-garde improvisations as he is with laying down a deep groove. He can be heard on releases by modern fuzoids Screaming Headless Torsos, saxophonist Steve Coleman, and trumpeter Roy Hargrove's RH Factor, as well as on releases by hip-hop artists D'Angelo, Maxwell, and Tricky.

Billy Kilson brought an urban edge to bassist Dave Holland's award-winning quintet on *Points Of View* in 1998, *Prime Directive* in 2000, 2001's *Not For Nothin'*, and 2003's *Extended Play: Live At Birdland*. He also appeared on the Dave Holland Big Band's 2002 release, *What Goes Around*.

Other hip-hop influenced drummers on the modern fusion scene include Terreon Gully, Chris "Daddy" Dave, Karriem Riggins, and New Orleans drummer Terence Higgins. Gully appeared on bassist Christian McBride's *Vertical Vision* in 2003 and 2004's *Evolution* by Stefon Harris & Blackout. Chris Dave has recorded with jazz saxophonist Kenny Garrett, gospel group Mint Condition, and R&B artists Mary J. Blige and Toni Braxton. Karriem Riggins has produced for Detroit hip-hop groups Common and Slum Village, and performed with a wide variety of jazz artists such as bassist Ray Brown, trumpeter Roy Hargrove, and pianist Mulgrew Miller. And Terence Higgins brought a hip-hop sensibility to the genre-bending music of The Dirty Dozen Brass Band.

Another modern jazz sub-genre, often referred to as "modern creative," blends elements of free improvisation, twentieth century classical, and other genres into a fresh and challenging new sound. New York City drummer Jim Black has been a major force in this micro-scene since joining saxophonist Tim Berne's Bloodcount in the early '90s. Black's stream-of-consciousness drumming style is highly interactive, rarely settling into repetitive patterns as he flows from one idea to the next. Other drummers associated with modern creative include Joey Baron, John

Hollenbeck, Susie Ibarra, Elliot Humberto Kavee, Bobby Previte, Tom Rainey, and Kenny Wollesen.

While Jim Black and his contemporaries have remained as underground heroes of contemporary avant-garde, other drummers have brought elements of the modern creative movement into mainstream jazz. Eric Harland and Nasheet Waits explored free-form concepts on releases by critically acclaimed pianist Jason Moran. Waits, who's a member of Moran's trio Bandwagon, has developed an innovation style that seamless blends post-bop vocabulary with open improvisation. Harland can be heard in a similar fashion on many recordings, including saxophonist Charles Lloyd's open-ended 2005 release, *Jumping The Creek*. Other drummers who have incorporated elements of free jazz drumming into their playing include Dave King with The Bad Plus, Ari Hoenig with pianists Kenny Werner and Jean-Michel Pilc, and Brian Blade with the Wayne Shorter Quartet.

## FURTHER LISTENING

**Miguel Zenón**
**Jíbaro** (Antonio Sanchez)

**Danilo Perez Trio**
**Live At The Jazz Showcase** (Adam Cruz)

**Dafnis Prieto**
**About The Monks** (Dafnis Prieto)

**Avishai Cohen**
**Adama** (Jeff Ballard)

**Kenny Garrett**
**Standard Of Language** (Eric Harland and Chris "Daddy" Dave)

**Tim Berne's Bloodcount**
**Unwound** (Jim Black)

**Susie Ibarra**
**Folkloriko** (Susie Ibarra)

**Fieldwork**
**Simulated Progress** (Elliot Humberto Kavee)

**Jason Moran**
**Same Mother** (Nasheet Waits)

**Wayne Shorter**
**Beyond The Sound Barrier** (Brian Blade)

## THE HISTORY OF MODERN DRUMMER MAGAZINE

### by Billy Amendola

Like many drummers, during my formative years I was a fan and loyal reader of *Modern Drummer* magazine. Founded in 1977 by publisher Ron Spagnardi, *MD* talked to us drummers with respect. This was *not* a small thing. Saddled with cliché jokes about lack of musical knowledge, drummers were routinely misunderstood—or worse, belittled—by the musical establishment. Then along came *Modern Drummer*, with intelligent, insightful interviews, challenging educational columns (often written by our drumming heroes!), and lots of great photographs. The world no longer could deny our contributions to music. We had found our voice. Largely, this could be attributed to the work of one man with a vision.

Ron Spagnardi was born on April 25, 1943. Following in the footsteps of his dad, Leo, who played drums in jazz and big bands in the '40s and '50s, Ron began showing an interest in playing when he was seven years old. Ron's wife, current *MD* publisher and CEO Isabel Spagnardi,

recalls, "He used to tell me that he would pull his dad's drums from the attic, set them up, play them, and have them back in the attic again before his dad came home from work. And his dad never knew it."

According to Isabel, at a very young age Ron also showed an interest in writing. "Ron was a drummer first, and also a fine piano/keyboard player. But he was also very good with words. Ever since he was six or seven, he would write stories. I have a scrapbook of his that's filled with his pieces."

Like most young musicians of the time, Ron paid his dues playing endless one-nighters. After graduating from Boston's Berklee College Of Music in 1963, Ron supplemented his earnings by giving music lessons and running his own music store in his hometown of Bloomfield, New Jersey.

After Ron and Isabel were married and had a daughter, Lori, spending time away from home became more difficult for him. Although he loved playing and was getting offers to go out with top acts, he was faced with a decision: life on the road, or following through on an idea that he had long kept in the back of his mind—an idea he'd been cooking up for a good *ten years* before he brought it up to his wife.

Isabel Spagnardi recalls the very first time her husband explained his vision to her. "It was the summer

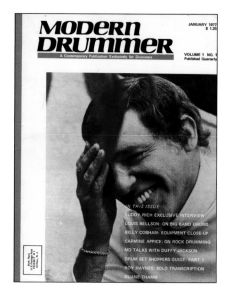

of 1974. Lori was about five years old at the time, and we were sitting in our backyard. Ron said, 'Is, I want to show you something. I have an idea.' So he hands me a prototype of a magazine. 'What's this?' 'It's a magazine for drummers,' he said. 'I feel that drummers don't have any publication that they can go to just for themselves. There's nothing around like it, but I feel it's a good idea and has a really good chance to go far.' I could tell he was excited."

Of course, at the time, the Spagnardis had no idea *how* far *Modern Drummer* would go. In a matter of months, what began as a single issue—with the modest hope of making back enough money to print a second one "sometime down the line"—would become renowned as the world's first and greatest serious drum publication, a distinction it retains thirty years on.

In 1974, however, such possibilities were the stuff of dreams, especially for a young couple of modest means. "When Ron first showed his prototype to me, I asked him, 'How much will this cost us?' When he told me I said, 'But Ron, that's practically *all* of our savings. I can think of

**The young publisher at his desk in 1977, and on the gig fifteen years earlier**

more important things we can spend that money on.' But luckily he persuaded me, and we went for it."

With no publication experience or big money behind him, Ron had to bank on what he *did* have: an in-depth knowledge of drums and drumming. Isabel remembers just how green the amateur publishers were: "Ron figured that we could advertise this as-yet-unpublished magazine in *Downbeat*, and in [local drummer Sam Ulano's newsletter] *Drum World*. What we didn't consider when we put the ads in the papers was that we were innocently breaking the law by advertising a product that didn't even exist yet."

The ads worked, though, and the subscriptions started coming in. Recalls Isabel, "It was Ron and I in the basement of our house, with a very old typewriter and a ping pong table to do layout on. But the phones started to ring. People had heard about the magazine, and they wanted it— even though we didn't even have our first issue out yet!"

*MD* senior vice president Lori Spagnardi recalls those very early days. "I was around six, and I remember helping my dad put the dummies together. He would have all the articles cut out, and he would let me put the rubber cement on the back. Then he would place them wherever he wanted to put them.

"He always wanted me involved, even at a young age," Lori continues. "I remember the excitement of that first issue coming off the press, and I still have this vision of staring at the box, and of him telling me that the first issue was red because that was my favorite color."

The concept of a magazine dedicated to drums and drummers clearly tapped into a widespread need in the music community. In less than two years, *Modern Drummer* grew to the point where it could no longer function "in the basement," and the

Spagnardis moved to their first proper office, at 1000 Clifton Ave. in Clifton, New Jersey. As the magazine got more popular and circulation grew, so did the staff, and in 1984, *MD* moved into a larger facility in nearby Cedar Grove, where it operated for the next ten years. In 1994, *MD* again moved, this time right down the road to a purpose-built complex that *MD*'s staffers—many of whom have been with the company for twenty years or more—still call home.

In the past three decades, every major international drummer has appeared in the pages of *Modern Drummer*. The magazine is available in dozens of countries around the world. It's known not just for its monthly flagship publication, but for a deep book-publishing division, a sister publication, *Drum Business*, and the premier drumming event in the world, the Modern Drummer Festival Weekend. Perhaps even more tellingly, *MD* boasts

years—long before he became my boss. He was a quiet, modest man who didn't like to publicly speak about his success. Whenever a reporter would call with a request to interview Ron, he would always say, "Why do they want to talk with *me*?" In a rare interview conducted by Bill Meligari, Ron was asked what he attributed *MD*'s success to. He replied, "I think the timing was right, and it filled a need. There were drummers out there who wanted something of their own, and no one was doing it. There were a couple of publications at the time, but they were created in-house by drum companies

## WE HAD FOUND OUR VOICE. THE WORLD COULD NO LONGER DENY OUR CONTRIBUTIONS TO MUSIC.

one of the most loyal readerships not only among music magazines, but in the entire magazine publishing industry. Quite a legacy for a man who really just wanted drummers to have their own voice.

No one knew Ron Spagnardi as well as his daughter. "My dad was a workaholic," shares Lori Spagnardi. "What I'll always remember and miss the most, though, is his amazing sense of humor. I could talk to him so easily—and sometimes without words. We just had to look at each other to know what the other was thinking."

I was among the fortunate people who got to know Ron Spagnardi well over the

specifically to advertise their own products and endorsers. We needed something that was going to talk about products across the board, something that would talk to *all* drummers."

Ron Spagnardi passed away on September 22, 2003. But the dream and vision he created will live on in the pages of *Modern Drummer*. Lori Spagnardi sums it up: "I know everyone here at *MD* shares his ideals. We all know how much this magazine meant to him, and what he wanted out of it. We'll do our best to continue his legacy."

# Index

Kirke, Simon, 61, 63
Knibbs, Lloyd, 113
Knox, Nick, 123
Kotche, Glenn, 87, 144
Kramer, Joey, 64, 164
Krauss, Scott, 87, 131
Kreutzmann, Bill, 158-159, 160
Krupa, Gene, 10-11, 34, 35, 37, 44, 60
Krusen, Dave, 148
Laboriel, Abe Jr., 72
Laine, George Vetiala "Papa Jack," 34
Lake, Gene, 167, 171
Lamond, Don, 40
Lampkin, Tyrone, 104
Lavis, Gilson, 123
Lawson, Ricky, 69
Lay, Sam, 53
LeBlanc, Keith, 166, 167
Lee, Tommy, 100
Leigh, Mike, 131
Leim, Paul, 77, 78, 79
Levey, Stan, 40
Lewis, Mel, 45
Lewis, Victor, 75, 129
Licht, David, 87
Liebezeit, Jaki, 86
Lind, Zach, 156
Lombardo, Dave, 164, 165
Londin, Larrie, 75
Lovering, David, 134
Lucas, Ray, 54
Ludwig, William, 36
Lynch, Stan, 64, 65
Maher, Fred, 87
Maher, John, 111
Mantilla, Ray, 126
Manne, Shelly, 42, 43, 44
Marine, Mitch, 69
Marotta, Jerry, 87
Marotta, Rick, 54, 75, 76
Mars, Chris, 134,
Marsh, Mike, 157
Marshall, Joseph "Kaiser," 34
Mason, Harvey, 77, 93, 104
Mason, Nick, 82
Massarella, Ben, 144
Mastelotto, Pat, 85
Mattacks, Dave, 75
Mayer, Jojo, 144, 167
McBrain, Nicko, 99, 101
McDonough, Matt, 164
McIntosh, Robbie, 104
McKinley, Ray, 35
Menza, Nick, 101
Merrick, 123
Miall, Terry Lee, 123
Miles, Buddy, 63
Mitchell, Mitch, 59, 62
Modeliste, Joseph "Zigaboo," 104, 105, 161
Moerlen, Pierre, 83
Moffet, Jonathan, 69
Moffit, Charles, 134
Moon, Keith, 18-19, 44, 45, 59, 62, 111, 121, 134, 135
Moore, Alan, 98
Moore, Cheron, 167
Moore, Oscar, 54

Moore, Stanton, 161
Moreira, Airto, 92, 95, 112, 117
Morello, Joe, 43, 45, 85
Morgenstein, Rod, 69
Morris, Stephen, 131
Mosely, Ian, 87
Motian, Paul, 42, 43, 75
Mouflet, Djoniba, 119
Mouzon, Alphonse, 92, 101
Moye, Don, 134
Muhammad, Idris, 53, 54, 75
Mullen, Larry Jr., 123
Murph, 134
Murray, Sunny, 134
Myers, Alan, 123
Myers, Kris, 161
Mysliwiec, Larry, 123
Nash, Lewis, 126, 128, 129
Nesbitt, Steve, 113
Newman, Tony, 63
Newmark, Andy, 75, 104
Nixon, Emmett, 166
Nkishi, Dodo, 144
Nolan, Jerry, 111
Novak, Gary, 69
Nussbaum, Adam, 129
Olatunji, Babtunde, 117
Oldaker, Jamie, 65
Olsson, Nigel, 62, 63
Otto, John, 164
Paice, Ian, 63, 97, 98, 141
Palmer, Carl, 83, 85, 101, 134
Palmer, Earl, 53, 72, 74
Parker, Chris, 75
Parker, Melvin, 54, 104
Parks, Deantoni, 167
Paul, Vinnie, 164, 165
Peart, Neil, 26-27, 65, 87, 101, 164
Pedersen, Chris, 134
Peebles, William, 54
Pelton, Shawn, 72, 75
Perkins, Stephen, 138-139, 141
Persip, Charlie, 53
Peters, Dan, 134, 148
Peterson, Ralph, 129
Phillips, Earl, 53
Phillips, Simon, 91, 92, 93, 98
Plourde, Derrick, 157
Porcaro, Jeff, 64, 65, 72, 74, 75, 92
Portnoy, Mike, 87, 101, 164
Pounds, Raymond, 104
Powell, Cozy, 68-69, 99
Pozo, Chano, 116, 170
Prescott, Peter, 134
Previte, Bobby, 171
Prieto, Dafnis, 170, 171
Prince, Prairie, 69
Puente, Tito, 95
Purdie, Bernard, 53, 54, 72, 75
Pyle, Pip, 83
Rabb, Johnny, 167
Rainey, Tom, 171
Rakha, Alla, 117
Ramone, Tommy, 111
Rebolo, George, 157
Reedus, Tony, 129
Reitzell, Brian, 87
Reyes, Walfredo de los, 95

Rich, Buddy, 12-13, 36, 44, 45, 62, 143
Richmond, Dannie, 45, 74
Rieflin, Bill, 87
Riggins, Karriem, 171
Riley, Ben, 45
Roach, Max, 37, 40, 42, 45, 126, 128, 150
Roberts, "Li'l" John, 105
Robinson, JR, 77, 104
Rockenfield, Scott, 87
Romao, Dom Um, 92, 95
Romweber, Sara, 134
Rose, Adonis, 153
Rose, Morgan, 165
Ross, Jorge, 153
Rudd, Phil, 65
Ruffy, Dave, 111
Russo, Joe, 161
Sales, Hunt, 68
Sanabria, Bobby, 95
Sanchez, Antonio, 75, 95, 168-169, 170, 171
Sandin, Eric, 156
Scabies, Rat, 110, 111
Schayer, Bobby, 156
Schock, Gina, 121, 123
Schrieve, Michael, 62, 117
Schwartzberg, Allan, 75
Seales, Sinclair, 113
Seraphine, Danny, 61, 64
Sery, Paco, 93
Sexton, Chad, 141
Shaughnessy, Ed, 65
Shelley, Steve, 133, 134
Shirley, Jerry, 63
Silveria, David, 164
Singleton, Zutty, 34
Siraisi, Genji, 167
Slade, Chris, 69
Smith, Chad, 136-137, 141
Smith, Marvin "Smitty," 128, 129
Smith, Steve, 93
Smith, Tony, 92
Smith, Warren, 126
Sneed, Floyd, 54
Sorum, Matt, 165
Spagnardi, Ron, 172
Starks, John "Jabo," 104
Starr, Ringo, 44, 59, 62, 82, 134
Stevenson, Bill, 108-109, 111
Stewart, Alonzo, 54
Stewart, Bill, 75, 152
Stubblefield, Clyde, 104, 150
Sturmer, Andy, 144
Takeishi, Satoshi, 117
Tate, Grady, 75
Taylor, Art, 43
Taylor, Roger, 62, 63
Taylor, Theresa, 134
Tempesta, John, 164
Theodore, Jon, 87, 144, 156
Thigpen, Ed, 45
Thomas, Jamal, 105
Thomas, Pete, 120, 123
Thompson, Ahmir "?uestlove," 166
Thompson, Chester, 93, 101
Thompson, Tony, 105
Thomson, Sebastian, 144

Tontoh, Frank, 105
Tough, Dave, 35, 37
Trainer, Todd, 87
Travis, Michael, 161
Travis, Scott, 98
Trucks, Butch, 62, 160, 161
Tucker, Maureen, 82, 134, 135
Tutt, Ron, 54
Ulrich, Lars, 164, 165
Valdez, Carlos "Patato," 95
Van Halen, Alex, 65, 99
Van Tieghem, David, 87
Vander, Christian, 83
Vasconcelos, Nana, 117
Vega, Carlos, 92
Verderosa, Tony, 167
Vincent, Alex, 147
Vrenna, Chris, 87
Wackerman, Chad, 86, 93
Wade, Adam, 144
Waits, Freddie, 126
Waits, Nasheet, 171
Walden, Narada Michael, 92, 101
Walford, Brit, 87
Walker, Jim, 131
Wallace, Winston "Horsemouth," 113
Waller, Mickey, 63
Ward, Bill, 98
Waronker, Joey, 69
Washam, Rey, 87
Washington, Kenny, 75, 128, 129
Watts, Charlie, 60, 63
Watts, Jeff "Tain," 75, 126, 128, 129, 151, 152
Weathers, John, 83
Webb, Chick, 32, 33, 34
Weckl, Dave, 92, 93, 94
Wellman, Ricky, 167
Welty, Ron, 156
Wertico, Paul, 93
White, Alan, 85
White, Fred, 104
White, Lenny, 92, 93
White, Maurice, 104
White, Meg, 156
Wilburn, Ishmael, 92
Wilk, Brad, 141, 164
Willard, Atom, 154-155, 157
Williams, Boris, 130, 131
Williams, James "Diamond," 104
Williams, Obie, 54
Williams, Tony, 16-17, 46, 47, 90, 91, 126, 128, 134, 150, 152, 153
Wilson, B.J., 75, 82
Wilson, Matt, 41, 153
Windsor, Morris, 134
Witten, Chris, 134
Wolleson, Kenny, 171
Woodyard, Sam, 43
Wyatt, Robert, 82, 83
Yamashta, Stomu, 83
Young, Adrian, 141
Young, Earl, 75
Zonder, Mark, 87
Zoro, 105

**ADAM BUDOFSKY** is the managing editor of *Modern Drummer* magazine.

**MICHELE M. HEUSEL** is the art director of *Modern Drummer* magazine.

**MICHAEL DAWSON** is associate editor at *Modern Drummer* magazine.

**MICHAEL PARILLO** is a writer, editor, and drummer. He's never stopped wishing he'd started playing earlier, but he's not using that as an excuse. Michael writes about music and food—two sides of the same coin, really—for a variety of print and online publications.

Margit Parillo

**MICHAEL BLAIR** has recorded and toured with Lou Reed, Elvis Costello, and Tom Waits, among many others.

Michael Kardas

**MEREDITH OCHS** is a music and popular culture commentator for National Public Radio's *All Things Considered*. She's also a contributing editor at *Guitar World* magazine and has written for *Entertainment Weekly*, *Rolling Stone*, and Salon.com, among others. Ochs hosts a daily show on Sirius Satellite Radio and is often heard on WFUV in New York City. She is the singer/songwriter/guitarist of The Damn Lovelys, who made their national debut on Mountain Stage.

**BILL MILLER** is editor in chief of *Modern Drummer* magazine.

**WILL ROMANO** has written for the New York *Post*, New York *Daily News*, *Modern Drummer*, *Guitar Player*, *FOH*, *Blues Revue*, *Goldmine*, *Military History*, and *Writer's Digest*. He is the author of *Incurable Blues: The Troubles And Triumph Of Blues Legend Hubert Sumlin* (Backbeat Books), and has just finished his second book, on the life and music of Jimmy Reed.

**JEFF POTTER** has contributed regularly to *Modern Drummer* magazine since 1985. His articles have also appeared in *Downbeat*, *Jazz Times*, *International Musician*, and *The New Grove Dictionary Of Jazz*. As a Broadway drummer, Potter continues his ten-year stint with *Rent* and is heard on the multi-platinum cast recording. His show-drumming career also includes performances with The Radio City Orchestra, national tours, recordings, and appearances on "Letterman" and "Leno" and in the movie *Camp* (IFC Films).

Lisa Walter

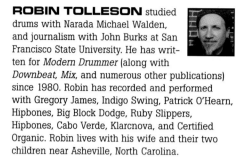

**ROBIN TOLLESON** studied drums with Narada Michael Walden, and journalism with John Burks at San Francisco State University. He has written for *Modern Drummer* (along with *Downbeat*, *Mix*, and numerous other publications) since 1980. Robin has recorded and performed with Gregory James, Indigo Swing, Patrick O'Hearn, Hipbones, Big Block Dodge, Ruby Slippers, Hipbones, Cabo Verde, Klarcnova, and Certified Organic. Robin lives with his wife and their two children near Asheville, North Carolina.

**KEN MICALLEF** used to perform for bar mitzvahs and weddings in the greater southeast US, but one day the monkey grinder removed his collar and set him free. Today, Ken contributes to *Mojo*, *Remix*, *Downbeat*, *Guitar One*, and of course, *Modern Drummer*.

**MIKE HAID** is a full-time contributing writer for *Modern Drummer* magazine and a freelance performing and recording drummer/vocalist based in Atlanta, Georgia. Mike is the former publisher of *Fuse* magazine, and has written for *Jazz Times*, *downbeat*, and *Mix*, among other major music publications. He is also a photographer, music producer, composer, arranger, engineer, graphic designer, father of three (Skylar, Jesse, Michael), and husband to one (Jeri).

**MARTIN PATMOS** grew up in Schenectady, New York, and graduated from the State University of New York at Oswego in 1995. Following college he continued studying jazz, ethnomusicology, and composition in New York City. Besides music and drumming, Martin enjoys hiking, cooking, and American history. Current projects include starting a jazz combo and teaching his four-year-old daughter to play drums. Patmos is a long-time contributor to *Modern Drummer* magazine.

**JON WURSTER** officially gave up baseball for drumming in the spring of 1981 when he joined his first band, Hair Club for Men. Since 1991, Wurster has been the drummer for indie-rock pioneers Superchunk; he has also recorded and toured with Jay Farrar, Ryan Adams, Rocket From The Crypt, R.E.M., Marah, and Robert Pollard. Wurster resides in Chapel Hill, North Carolina.

**WALEED RASHIDI** has been immersed in drums for over two decades. He's toured throughout North America, Japan, and Europe, and has credits on over a dozen releases. As a freelance journalist, Waleed has penned features for *Modern Drummer*, *VW Driver*, *Alternative Press*, *E! Online*, and *Alarm*. Formerly the editor in chief of *Mean Street* magazine, Waleed is currently the art director of *Dispatch* and teaches college courses part-time. When he isn't slamming his 2002s and Maple

Customs, Waleed can be found tinkering with his many mopeds (yes, the ones with pedals).

**MATT WILSON** leads his own jazz groups, and plays with Dewey Redman, Lee Konitz, Andrew Hill, and Buster Williams, among other top jazz artists.

**DAVID LICHT** was born in Detroit and raised in Greensboro, North Carolina, where he studied with jazz drummer Sammy Anflick. He met guitar wildman Eugene Chadbourne at The Creative Music Studio in Woodstock in 1978 and soon became part of The Chadbournes, which morphed into the legendary psychedelic comedy band Shockabilly. Licht moved to New York City in 1985 to manage the recording studio Noise New York, and helped form another famed band, Bongwater, with producer/genius (Mark) Kramer. Licht later became a founding member of The Klezmatics, who are still active today. David has been a painter/plasterer/faux finisher for over thirty years, and lives in New Jersey with his occupational therapist wife, Karen, and his two kids, Jacob and Bess.

**VICTOR DELORENZO** is the drummer with Violent Femmes, leader of his own projects, Marcel Duchamp champion, and owner-operator of The Past Office recording studio/salon.

**STANTON MOORE** is the drummer/leader of Galactic, and has worked with Robert Walter, Garage A Trois, and Corrosion Of Conformity.

**BILLY AMENDOLA** is associate editor at *Modern Drummer* magazine.

### THE MODERN DRUMMER STAFF

**Isabel Spagnardi**, publisher/CEO
**Kevin W. Kearns**, vice president
**Tracy A. Kearns**, associate publisher
**Lori Spagnardi**, senior vice president
**Rick Van Horn**, senior editor
**Suzanne Hurring**, editorial assistant
**Scott G. Bienstock**, senior art director
**Gerald Vitale Jr.**, assistant art director
**Bob Berenson**, advertising director.
**Joan C. Stickel**, advertising assistant
**Rosemary Blaha**, office assistant

The editor would like to thank the following drummers: Jaki Liebezeit, Michael Parillo, Michael Dawson, Chad Smith, Michael Blair, Victor DeLorenzo, Brian Reitzell, and David Licht. And, the drummers who might not know a paradiddle from a papa relleno, but who are *just* as inspirational: Meredith Ochs, Jennifer Schwartz, Elizabeth Walsh—and especially Susanne, Luca, Hayden, and Jack Budofsky. Thank you also to the *Modern Drummer* writers and staff, including senior art director Scott Bienstock and associate publisher Tracy Kearns, but most of all Michele Heusel, for your constant support and patience.

**For Keith Moon and Ron Spagnardi.**